THE

ADOLESCENT

JOURNEY

An Interdisciplinary Approach

to Practical Youth Ministry

AMY E. JACOBER

IVP Books

An imprint of InterVarsity Press
Downers Grove, Illinois

InterVarsity Press
P.O. Box 1400, Downers Grove, IL 60515-1426
World Wide Web: www.ivpress.com
E-mail: email@ivpress.com

InterVarsity Press® is the book-publishing division of InterVarsity Christian Fellowship/USA®, a movement of students and faculty active on campus at hundreds of universities, colleges and schools of nursing in the United States of America, and a member movement of the International Fellowship of Evangelical Students. For information about local and regional activities, write Public Relations Dept., InterVarsity Christian Fellowship/USA, 6400 Schroeder Rd., P.O. Box 7895, Madison, WI 53707-7895, or visit the IVCF website at <www.intervarsity.org>.

All Scripture quotations, unless otherwise indicated, are taken from the Holy Bible, New International Version®. NIV®. Copyright ©1973, 1978, 1984 by International Bible Society. Used by permission of Zondervan Publishing House. All rights reserved.

While all stories in this book are true, some names and identifying information in this book have been changed to protect the privacy of the individuals involved.

Design: Cindy Kiple

Interior design: Beth Hagenberg

Images: Valentino Sani/Trevillion Images

ISBN 978-0-8308-3418-1

Printed in the United States of America ∞

Library of Congress Cataloging-in-Publication Data

Jacober, Amy.
   The adolescent journey: an interdisciplinary approach to practical
youth ministry/Amy Jacober.
     p. cm.
   Includes bibliographical references (p.).
   ISBN 978-0-8308-3418-1 (pbk.: alk. paper)
   1. Church work with teenagers. 2. Theology, Practical. I. Title.
   BV4447.J24 2011
   259'.23—dc22

2010052958

P	19	18	17	16	15	14	13	12	11	10	9	8	7	6	5	4	3	2	1
Y	26	25	24	23	22	21	20	19	18	17	16	15	14	13	12	11

CONTENTS

INTRODUCTION

GROWING UP AND SO MANY PLACES TO GO!

Our mission is to convey God's love—not a dead God but a living God, a God of love.

MOTHER TERESA

A BOWL OF PEAS FOR YOUR birthright: with the benefit of hindsight, this seems like a ridiculous trade. But in the moment, it can seem like a perfectly reasonable exchange.

This particular moment involved two people with a complicated relationship. They were twin brothers, but they didn't have much in common: Esau, older by a nose, a hunter—busy, hardworking—who spent most of his time roaming the desert; and Jacob, a gardener and gatherer who tended to keep to himself in his own fields. Still, Jacob had tried his best to be born first—he came out of the womb grasping his brother's heel.

We might imagine them as teenagers. When both were doing what they did best and leaving the other alone, the arrangement worked. But you can only ignore and avoid your adolescent siblings for so long. And on one particular occasion, Esau came home from the wild full of stories, exhausted, hungry. Jacob, meanwhile, had remained home and prepared a meal.

Jacob: "Hey. What's up?"
Esau: "Grunt. Give me some of that."
Jacob: "No way. Get your own!"

Esau: "Come on, man! I'm starving! I'm gonna die if I don't get some-
    thing to eat!"
Jacob: "Hmmm, in that case . . . What's it worth to you?"
Esau: "Are you kidding me? Just give me some stew."
Jacob: "No way. I slaved over this. You need to give me something in
    return."
Esau: "I don't have anything to give you! I couldn't catch anything
    today. Why do you think I'm so hungry?"
Jacob: "Well then, no stew for you."
Esau: "OK, fine. What do you want?"
Jacob: "How about your birthright?"

Esau, tired and overwhelmed, goes for the immediate gratification,
sells his birthright and settles down for a satisfying bowl of lentil stew
(Genesis 25:27-34).

Maybe you've told this story to your youth group. Maybe you've
warned them that studies show that kids who can't delay gratification
suffer as adults. Maybe you silently wondered why Jacob was such a
jerk, and hoped none of your students would ask why God let him get
away with it. In any case, you probably never thought of yourself, as a
youth minister, being like Esau. But if you're like many youth ministers, you're more like Esau than you'd like to think.

Most youth ministers wouldn't be tempted by a bowl of peas, but
there are many other things that would catch us in Jacob's trap. What,
for example, is the role (or the birthright) of the youth minister? As
we'll see in the pages that follow, the youth minister's role at its heart is
to join God in his work of reconciliation in the world. And yet too often
youth ministers are lured away from this birthright by the latest games,
the newest music or DVD, counseling techniques, a bestselling curriculum, an evangelism program, social activism . . . The list could go
on and on and on.

Youth ministers are not that far from Esau, actually. We begin with
the best of intentions and end tired, seeking immediate gratification.
Our time goes to leaders and adolescents; we run from staff meetings
to basketball games to the local hangout. And then when it comes time

to pray, lead a group, teach on Sunday, give a talk or plan a retreat—let alone have a one-on-one conversation with one of our students—we are weary.

And that's how it is for those of us who are lucky enough to have a full-time ministry position. According to a Barna Research study, only one in five youth ministers in Protestant churches is a full-time paid minister. Four of every five are bivocational or volunteer—working full time somewhere else (or finishing academic degrees).[1] We don't have time for our birthright, and we lose sight of its value.

Even if we hold tight to our birthright, often our churches trade it right out from under us. That many churches would pass over a youth worker with a firm grasp of theology in order to hire one who knows how to manage budgets, create promotional materials and keep a program running is plainly evident from a survey of web postings for youth ministry jobs. We have been taught both formally and through expectations of the church (or parachurch or other Christian organizations) that it is better to throw a good party with a lot of adolescents than to intentionally enter into ministry with one. A common conversation in the last five years has centered on the outcomes of the National Study of Youth and Religion. In particular is Christian Smith's term "Moral Therapeutic Deism."[2] Years ago I was criticized rather sharply by a well-known youth speaker for being too harsh in stating that we seem to be raising a generation that is biblically illiterate and theologically void. I did not say this with any amount of joy or arrogance, rather with deep concern and heartache. Years later, Kenda Dean affirmed this assessment with much more

---

[1]"Pastors Paid Better, but Attendance Unchanged," Barna Research Online, March 29, 2001, accessed January 31, 2003 <www.barna.org/barna-update/article/5-barna-update/39-pastors-paid-better-but-attendance-unchanged?q=pastors+paid+better>. Barna does not use standard methodological practices as accepted by academic researchers, but this study is the best source available for such a question as this. This may be compared with youth workers in general under research accessed November 27, 2010, at <www.cornerstones4kids.org> under "resources and links" then "youth development." "Growing the Next Generation of Youth Professionals: Workforce, Opportunities and Challenges," prepared by Nicole Yohalem, Karen Pittman and David Moore.

[2]See Christian Smith and Melinda Lundquist Denton, *Soul Searching: The Religious and Spiritual Lives of American Teenagers* (New York: Oxford University Press, 2005).

than my gut feeling. She states that our teens practice Moral Therapeutic Deism "not because they have misunderstood what we have taught them in church. *They practice it because this is what we have taught them in church.*"[3] Without realizing it, youth ministers—and churches and ministries alongside them—model Esau, asking the nearest available Jacob questions like "Is there a lesson I can prepare in thirty minutes or less?" "Is there some video clip I can show to make me look like I know what's going on in the world today?" "I have a student in crisis; what would a social worker do?" "What song or movie can I name-drop to get the kids' attention?"

There are more than enough resources out there for all these questions and more. But the more we come to rely on them, the more and more of our birthright we're outsourcing, and the less and less actual ministry we're doing.

It took years for Jacob and Esau to be reconciled. Esau regretted his foolish decisions, made in the moment, and he resented Jacob for taking his birthright from him. We don't hear from him in the Bible for a long stretch of time. But eventually we're reintroduced to him, and when these brothers meet again, Esau embraces Jacob, and the family is restored.

Reconciliation is the work of God in the world. It is the longing of Jesus to be in right relationship with each of us and that we be in right relationship with each other. "So if anyone is in Christ, there is a new creation: everything old has passed away; see everything has become new! All this is from God, who reconciled us to himself through Christ, and has given us the ministry of reconciliation; that is, in Christ God was reconciling the world to himself, not counting their trespasses against them, and entrusting the message of reconciliation to us" (2 Corinthians 5:17-19 NRSV). Sometimes this means having to reconcile issues in our own lives as we seek to be healthy and whole, and sometimes it means identifying and working to change systems and structures that inhibit efforts at reconciliation. Reconciliation doesn't just

---

[3]Kenda Creasy Dean, *Almost Christian: What the Faith of Our Teenagers Is Telling the American Church* (New York: Oxford University Press, 2010), p. 29, italics in original.

happen. It takes time and effort. Even more, it takes the transformative work of Jesus himself.

For example, the reconciliation that eventually occurs between Jacob and Esau comes after life experience. In scene upon scene we observe Jacob finding God and God's purposes behind his own actions and circumstances. Indeed, Jacob observes a "ladder to heaven," and the comings and goings of God's agents among human affairs. He himself wrestles God and feels the effects long after being granted God's blessing. By the time Jacob is reunited with Esau, he sees the birthright he stole from his brother not as a privilege but as a way of life. He has himself been reconciled to God, and armed with God's blessing he creatively and humbly pursues reconciliation with his brother.

We might, in this sense, begin to think of Jacob as a practical theologian, and his reconciliation with his brother the ministry that pours out of his theology. Practical theology takes place when human experience and theological reflection intermingle. It has special value in bringing reconciliation to volatile contexts, which adolescence surely counts as. This book will explore the ways in which youth ministers can function as practical theologians as they help students navigate the difficult passage from childhood to adulthood, where new situations force theological reflection and theology forces a new way of seeing and responding to a real-life situation.

Youth ministry over the years has put much emphasis on studying, analyzing and learning adolescent culture. This work has often been motivated by a desire to better minister to adolescents. Yet in the process youth ministers have traditionally not been encouraged to take theology seriously. Thankfully this is changing. Whereas most youth ministry publications over its roughly one-hundred-year history compartmentalized theological and psychosocial frameworks,[4] much recent youth min-

---

[4]Allen Jackson, "Does the Church Need Youth Ministry?" *American Baptist Quarterly* 19, no. 1 (March 2000): 41-42. Robert Raikes started his Sunday school in England in 1780. In 1824 the American Sunday School Union was formed in Philadelphia. In 1881 Francis Clark started the Society for Christian Endeavor for young people to grow in their walk with God. In 1891 both the Presbyterian Westminster League and a national Baptist young people's organization were formed. In 1893 the Walther League (Missouri Synod Lutheran) and in 1895 the

istry literature emphasizes the integrative work of practical theology.[5] This comes in part as a result of the longstanding concern over "irrelevant theorists and mindless practitioners"[6]—that what is being taught within the walls of colleges and seminaries has no application once the minister enters the world of local ministry. David Livermore says, "The best choice for preparing youth ministers cannot be to decide between theory and practice. Theory and practice, or engagement and reflection, also known as praxis, are needed simultaneously."[7]

Andrew Root suggests that "why youth ministry matters and is important" needs to be considered "from a biblical and cultural perspective."[8] In a generation that is, in general, biblically illiterate and theologically untrained,[9] there are nevertheless theological questions unique to the adolescent experience, and in fact unique to the adolescent experience in this particular historical moment.[10] As Duncan Forrester suggests, adolescents are not only unique but also constantly changing, so that adolescents today are quite different from adolescents thirty years ago. Asking contextual questions about the contemporary adolescent and contemporary adolescence, and sorting through the response within the adolescent context, is itself theological.[11]

Luther League (Lutheran) joined as well.

[5]Most notably Dean Borgman, *When Kumbya Is Not Enough: A Practical Theology for Youth Ministry* (Peabody, Mass.: Hendrickson, 1997); Kenda Creasy Dean, Chap Clark and Dave Rahn, eds., *Starting Right: Thinking Theologically About Youth Ministry* (Grand Rapids: Zondervan, 2001); Kenda Creasy Dean, "The New Rhetoric of Youth Ministry," *Journal of Youth and Theology* 2, no. 2 (2003).

[6]David Livermore, "The Youth Ministry Education Debate: Irrelevant Theorists Versus Mindless Practitioners," *The Journal of Youth Ministry* 1, no. 1 (Fall 2002): 89-102.

[7]Ibid., p. 94.

[8]Andrew Root, *Revisiting Relational Youth Ministry: From a Strategy of Influence to a Theology of Incarnation* (Downers Grove, Ill.: InterVarsity Press, 2007).

[9]See Christian Smith and Melinda Denton, *Soul Searching* (New York: Oxford University Press, 2005), for a clearly spelled out and thoroughly researched explanation of this concept.

[10]E-mail exchange between Duncan Forrester and the author. To my (and his) knowledge this has not yet been done to this extent, so it is not an update but rather an (at times clumsy) effort to establish an intentional focus on youth ministry from within the field of practical theology. What I am proposing is certainly focused on adolescents but specifically from within practical theology.

[11]I am aware of the temptation to create something in order to justify my own exis-

Three related insights set the stage for the reconciliation ministry that is the youth worker's birthright. First, *youth workers must be bilingual—* able to find correspondence between the asymmetrical perspectives of social psychology and theology. The theoretical and practical issues that attend to adolescence are best considered in the light of both these disciplines and in their correspondence. Second, *a practical theology of youth ministry unites three strands of existence: the individual, the communal and the eternal.* Acknowledgment and synthesis of these three are crucial in the major life task of adolescence. Third, a maturing adolescent is nurtured *through the transformative power of Christ* and *the commingling virtues of love, justice and mercy.* This book will unpack each part and show both their relation to one another and to youth ministry.

Theology takes time and effort. A lack of focus on this has resulted in a plethora of well-intended, sincere-hearted but shallow-at-best and dangerous-at-worst teachings and leadings across denominational lines. *It is important to note that it is not because youth ministers are incapable or lazy.* Rather, in the fast-paced world of the dynamic lives of adolescents, youth ministers find themselves lacking in time, skills, knowledge and a point of entry to do much beyond what they are already doing.

Theology was never intended to be an irrelevant exercise in academic gymnastics. It is our faith, guided by the questions of our day, seeking understanding from God. For the youth minister, these are the questions which arise from looking closer at the lives and culture of the adolescents whom we are called to serve, whom we love and whom we know.

---

tence. Ray Anderson best put words to my fears when he wrote, "Has theology succumbed totally to the prevailing winds of praxis, where movements write their conceptual basis for existence as revolutionary manifestos meant to justify as much as to compel? Or to put it another way, does a political theology or a black theology appropriate revelation to a concrete situation in such a way that the immediate occasion becomes the authoritative "text"? Has theology virtually become hermeneutics— where self understanding incorporates the data of revelation into one's own experience and action?" Ray Anderson, *The Shape of Practical Theology: Empowering Ministry with Theological Praxis* (Downers Grove, Ill.: InterVarsity Press, 2001), p. 61. The hermeneutical depth of a particular view is always in danger of becoming the text instead of the context.

YOUTH MINISTRY AS PRACTICAL THEOLOGY

TRINITARIAN, CHRISTOCENTRIC, TRANSFORMATIONAL

True theology is practical; speculative theology belongs to the devil in hell.

MARTIN LUTHER

MOST OF MY YEARS AS A student were spent being told, then reminded, then encouraged to ponder that God loved me and Jesus died for me. Discipleship and doctrines beyond salvation were mentioned but were not the focus. Spiritual formation and my responsibility toward this world and other people as a Christian were clearly not priorities.

College didn't move me any closer to knowing the bigger picture of what it meant to be a Christian. I faltered around and did the best I could talking about Jesus while folding clothes at the Gap or praying with someone who just got dumped at an after-hours dance party. While I am sure my experience wasn't the case for everyone, I do not think it was as unique as I wish it was.

Then I went to seminary, where I realized that while I could find Scriptures with a concordance, I lacked context or doctrinal understanding and the ability to think Christianly. I was embarrassed more often than not, but I finally decided it was better to be embarrassed and ask lots of questions than to keep playing the good Christian hoping I wouldn't get caught for how little I knew. Once I had some theological categories down, I hoped, ministry would be easy; and if not easy, at least I hoped I would have some kind of direction. I overestimated what it meant to have theology "down"; I needed a way to translate the theology I could now articulate into real life.

For me, social work let me put flesh on my theological bones. I assumed I would have students requiring these skills only periodically, but the longer I served in youth ministry, the more my skills in social work became relevant. At the churches where I have been on staff and in other ministries, only a handful of my students would be considered "healthy." Instead I was led to adolescents (or they were led to me) who were drug-using, lying, Wiccan-practicing, abused, gang-affiliated, marginalized, poverty-stricken and serial foster-care children—not to mention the usual suspects of issues present in an adolescent life. I was frequently overwhelmed, working hard and looking for what could get one of these teenagers (and me) to the next day. I was more than willing to ask any Jacob I could find for short-term fulfillment, forgetting that long-term sustenance was the goal.

Social work, a point of God-given passion for me, took over my role as youth worker, but this is not the only area where a youth worker can lose his or her primary identity. The entertainer, the cultural guru, the game master, the trip planner could all be inserted and sought after where I placed social work. The results of these ambitions as a focus are more immediate, providing instant gratification. Ironically what I learned in studying social work is that there are many social workers, teachers, coaches, counselors, musicians—a whole host of people who do what they do much better than a youth minister can. Most of them are not trying to be ministers, and yet as ministers, we do try to be them.

These days, in my work with students I still do a lot of informal social work, but I now recognize my priority in doing what youth workers can do best in the lives of their students: theology.

COMMONALITY AND DIFFERENCE

It is fair to say youth ministers want to honor God, share Christ, minister to adolescents and their families, and not only personally live a

Christian life but lead others to do so as well. In pursuit of that goal, youth ministers seem to have a mystical ability to transcend controversial divisions, denominational litmus tests and personal preference in the name of collaborating with others who love God and teenagers as much as they do. This is evidenced by the many conferences and events held each year in the United States and around the world, where thousands upon thousands of youth and adult youth leaders come together to praise God and learn more about serving Jesus in and among teenagers.

There is, however, a potentially negative side of youth workers bypassing differences. Theological convictions often take a back seat to cooperation, leaving theological convictions necessarily shallow. Bible studies written for a broad swath of theological traditions give little to no consideration of theological heritage. Conferences are planned and executed without regard to the particular cultural issues present in the intended audience. Too often, tradition-defining doctrinal positions are abandoned in the name of collaboration.

A balance is needed. We begin to approach that balance when we begin to consider our context.

The questions that plague adolescents are constantly changing, as much as adolescents change themselves. Youth ministers have worked hard to discover and express these questions with each passing generation. In fact, the struggle comes not as much with youth ministry's relevance but with our substance—our understanding of holistic adolescent development and its implications for holistic youth ministry.

Over the years holistic adolescent development has been an emphasis in youth ministry, but relevancy—finding the latest theme, song or program—has been the dominant focus. The priority of relevancy has even driven the contemporary focus on spirituality, simplicity and a hearkening back to ancient practices. When it comes to the day-to-day details of a youth ministry, substance—engaging adolescents as whole persons with the whole gospel—can fall by the wayside.[1]

---

[1]One notable exception to this is Fernando Arzola, *Toward a Prophetic Youth Ministry: Theory and Praxis in Urban Context* (Downers Grove, Ill.: InterVarsity Press, 2008).

Without maintaining substance as our guiding principle, we can lose sight of the answer to the question "What really constitutes 'Christian'?"[2] This question subdivides into the question whether theology is a transforming or descriptive discipline, and the challenge of avoiding the twin perils of Christian faith—becoming (a) solely a private affair with no effect in the public arena or (b) a public action with no individual understanding.[3]

THE NEED FOR A PRACTICAL THEOLOGY OF YOUTH MINISTRY

I was approached a few years ago by a seminary-trained, veteran youth minister (working with other veteran, trained youth ministers) who said he had a great theme for a camp experience, where students would leave on fire for Christ and ready to share the gospel with everyone. He came up with the idea while at the House of Blues, the logo for which is a heart on fire. T-shirts were already ordered with the Scripture Luke 24:32: "Were not our hearts burning within us while he talked with us on the road and opened the Scriptures to us?" He wanted me to create the curriculum.

It is not unusual to have inspiration come from a rather mundane moment in life. Nevertheless, the Scripture they had arrived at does not imply the great evangelistic thrust they were assuming. It had all the right words—*hearts, burning*—but an entirely different meaning.

As the t-shirts were already printed, I suggested that we keep the theme and Scripture but remain true to the text—that we explore how we often look for God to show up in the way we are hoping and expect-

[2]Jim McClendon emphasizes the question "What is really Christian?" in response to what has become a common (at best tolerant, at worst pluralistic) approach to the Christian world mission. James Wm. McClendon Jr., *Systematic Theology*, vol. 2, *Doctrine* (Nashville: Abingdon, 1994), p. 420. Other thinkers who have contributed in small and larger ways have been Walter Rauschenbusch, Jimmy Carter, Friedrich Schleiermacher, Derrel Watkins, Diana Garland, David Gil, Mother Teresa, Dietrich Bonhoeffer, Duane K. Friesen, Michael Walzer, Robert Bellah, Stanley Hauerwas and Nelson Mandela. In addition have been a whole host of personal friends with whom I have spent hours peering at every facet of this issue only to find that as the light shifted, another facet was revealed.
[3]For further discussion of similar questions and more, see John Howard Yoder's *For the Nations: Essays Public and Evangelical* (Eugene, Ore.: Wipf & Stock, 2002).

ing, and because we're not open to how God chooses to manifest, we miss his presence. The theme worked, and the students went home with a new appreciation for God's activity in their lives—even when they don't realize it.

It *is* possible to be relevant to young people *and* true to the Scriptures. We accomplish these goals when we keep the priorities of practical theology in the foreground, when we carefully study our context and then carefully reflect on the Scriptures, and seek to reconcile the two. In a word, a ministry of practical theology requires that we be *bilingual.*

THE BILINGUAL DIALOGUE

Practical theology is neither merely applied theology nor pragmatic application with a prayer. It is, rather, a dialogue between traditional theological approaches, on the one hand, and psychosocial perspectives, on the other, regarding the context we find ourselves in.

Paulo Freire describes two characteristics of the word *dialogue* which are of particular interest here. Dialogue is composed of reflection and action. If reflection is lacking, the undertaking is diminished to mere activism. If action is neglected, the undertaking becomes idle chatter.[4] As indicated by Deborah van Deusen Hunsinger, this dialogue is more rigorous than the instinctual approach that dominates ministry.[5] It requires a look at who we are as humans and who we are as spiritual beings.

Hunsinger uses a Barthian interpretation of the Chalcedonian pattern to present the idea of asymmetry between the divine and human nature. She takes her premise from George Hunsinger:

> The two natures are not conceived as ordered, according to a scale whereby they would differ only in degree. [Rather they are] conceived as asymmetrically related, for they share no common measure or standard of measurement. Although there is a divine

---

[4]Paulo Freire, *Pedagogy of the Oppressed*, trans. Myra Bergman Ramos (New York: Continuum, 1989), p. 19.
[5]Deborah van Deusen Hunsinger, *Theology and Pastoral Counseling: A New Interdisciplinary Approach* (Grand Rapids: Eerdmans, 1995).

priority and human subsequence, their asymmetry allows a conception which avoids hierarchical domination in favor of a mutual ordering of freedom.[6]

For Deborah Hunsinger, this concept of asymmetry means that the pastoral counselor will be fluent in both theology and psychology without attempting to translate them into one another.[7] Psychology is not made Christian simply by shoring it up with a prayer or a proof text. Neither is Christianity made psychologically sound by adding a few counseling techniques to what is otherwise a theological exercise. A bilingual approach to youth ministry requires taking both assymetrical languages seriously and allowing them to function within the realm for which they were created. So a practical theology of youth ministry seeks to be conceptually adequate when looking at the divine mystery in the lives of adolescents.

If theology is a language, then the other language required of the bilingual practical theologian is determined by context. For the context of youth ministry, the second language takes into consideration issues of adolescent development in a particular cultural setting.[8] The adolescent is a whole person, of course—not to be divided in her spiritual life from her psychosocial life. That being said, the spiritual cannot be *confused* with the psychosocial.[9] Jesus Christ is fully divine and fully human; yet it is often the case that the dual nature of Christ is accepted with an elevation of the divine. This manner of a preference might imply at best a compartmentalism of sorts and at worst docetism or a modified gnosticism where Jesus was not *fully* human.[10] Similarly, adolescent development and cultural

---

[6]George Hunsinger, *How to Read Karl Barth: The Shape of His Theology* (New York: Oxford University Press, 1991), pp. 286-87 n. 1.

[7]Hunsinger, *Theology and Pastoral Counseling*, p. 64.

[8]There are a number of disciplines which contribute heavily to my understanding of adolescence in context: social work, sociology, cultural studies/anthropology and psychology. Other disciplines might be similarly significant to other youth workers.

[9]This has been further refined through James Loder. His contribution will be made clear in the upcoming chapters.

[10]There is another point of contention in accepting the dual nature of Christ from a creedal perspective. Conciliar orthodoxy offers the divine impassibility of Christ as

hermeneutics are not to be placed in hierarchical priority above or below theology; they are entirely different from theology and ought to be guarded as such.

INFLUENCES

While my theological background is Baptist, practical theology never claims to present strict doctrine or dogma. Hence the practical theology offered in this book could work with a variety of traditions. James Wm. McClendon Jr. offers the image of a three-strand rope.[11] The rope is composed of three strands with no center core. Each of the strands (or "facets") is individual in essence; together they constitute the rope. No strand can act alone or do what the rope does apart from the other two. The rope as well does not exist apart from the presence of all three strands intertwined to create the rope.[12]

McClendon has called one strand the body, one strand the social and one strand the resurrection.[13] These strands look at ways in which we as Christians find ourselves as

1) part of the natural order, organic beings, bodies in an organic continuum, God's natural creation; but also 2) part of a social world that is constituted first by the corporate nature of Christian existence, the church, and thereby our share in human society, God's social creation, as well; and 3) part of an eschatological realm, the kingdom of God, the "new world" established by God's resurrection of Jesus of Nazareth from the dead.[14]

---

a dogma. In order to do this, however, one must accept that God suffers in Godself and not just in Christ's humanity, thus denying the accepted Chalcedonian definition. To hold to doctrine based on creeds can lead to unintentional contradictions. As a Baptist, many of the same tenets are held but for very different reasons and accepted after following a different path.

[11]In this McClendon modifies a Wittgensteinian image; see Ludwig Wittgenstein, *Philosophical Investigations,* trans. G. E. M. Anscombe (New York: Macmillan, 1953), p. 67. I refer to the "strands" as "facets" to emphasize the particular validity of each as well as the greater whole from which they may not be separated.

[12]James Wm. McClendon Jr., *Systematic Theology,* vol. 1, *Ethics* (Nashville: Abingdon, 1986), p. 64.

[13]Ibid., p. 66.

[14]Ibid.

I take McClendon's "natural order" to refer to the individual in a holistic developmental perspective. This includes a spiritual account of development as well as a biological and social for each person.

In Genesis 1, God created humanity in his image, male *and* female (*not* male *or* female). The image of God is communal. I take the second strand, consequently, to refer to the communal. We do not exist within a vacuum, and as much as there is an individual component to life, we are never isolated entirely. We are communal not only with one another in our communities, both near and far, here on earth but also with God the Father, Son and Holy Spirit.

The third strand, McClendon's "new world," refers to the reality that our development and lives in this time and place have eternal implications both for ourselves as individuals and for those around us.

These three strands, then—the individual, the communal and the eternal—will constitute the basis of this practical theology.

FOCUS

Practical theology—a bilingual endeavor that creates space for a needed dialogue—is not only possible but also appropriate, based on the precedent that Jesus himself adapted his message. Duncan Forrester reminds us that Jesus

> didn't say the same thing, or call for the same response from the woman at the well as from the rich young ruler! In youth ministry we do not say the same thing as we do to the elderly, like me! And it is so important to listen, so that we are not answering questions that no one is asking![15]

Youth ministry has the happy burden of not only discovering and deciphering the questions being asked by an often misunderstood and neglected population, but also the privilege of offering a focused response of reconciliation.

This book will walk through the formation and application of a practical theology of youth ministry. Chapter two, "Practical Theol-

---

[15]E-mail from Duncan Forrester to the author, August 23, 2002.

ogy: A Christocentric Practice," sets up the template in general. Chapter three, "Overlapping Spheres in Adolescent Development: Healthy Individuation," explores the first half of the psychosocial language specifically (though not exclusively) with an individual focus. Chapter four, "A Clarification of Context: Understanding Youth Culture," shifts to the second half of the psychosocial language specifically (though again not exclusively) with a communal focus.

Chapter five, "Theological Influences: Faith with Understanding," explores the second language specifically though not exclusively with an eternal focus. Chapter six, "A Depth Encounter with Central Virtues: Love, Mercy, Justice and Transformation," considers the existence of three central virtues transcending all three strands by the transformative power of Christ.

The construction of a practical theology of youth ministry requires a strong ability for interdisciplinary thought. The result of this construction guides youth ministers to intentionally join God in his work of transformation, stepping away from the quick fix and reclaiming our birthright as we recognize God's patient work in our lives and those around us!

QUESTIONS FOR FURTHER THOUGHT

1. What do you personally focus on that can push being a "minister" to the back seat?

2. What theological influences are you able to identify in your own life? How and where do these influences show up in your beliefs? In your actions?

2

PRACTICAL THEOLOGY

A CHRISTOCENTRIC PRACTICE

ADULTS ARE HYPOCRITES." I hear things like this all the time from teenagers. "I'm told to control my temper, but I see my dad flip off other drivers on the freeway." "Everyone says I need to 'commit to Jesus' and my church, but my parents have us skip all the time for camping, beach trips or a big game." "My parents and you tell me to keep myself pure, but I know my mom sneaks off and smokes pot when she gets head-aches or stressed. Is that what she means by pure?" "I get so many mixed messages. I hear people say to do my homework and do well in school, but I have teachers who don't like me. I mean really don't like me—they say that I'll never amount to anything and should give up now so I stop wasting their time." I've even had students confess to me that they feel guilty for all their youth pastor expects from them and angry because they know he doesn't do half of what he says. These are not made up situations; these are all real from over the years and around the country as I have been privileged to serve. For those of us in youth ministry, it is a frustrating tide of contradiction.

Here's the hard part for many of us to hear: we say, "Treat others as Jesus would," and yet our humor is sarcastic and hurts others. We say, "Let's care for the poor," but we walk by them if a teenager isn't with us. We say, "Jesus does not condone violence," but we make a weekly tour-nament around killing, stealing and beating the living daylights out of each other through characters in a video game. We say, "Take care of your body as the temple of Christ," but we buy junk food for every youth group event. We say, "Spend time praying and reading Scripture," and we can't remember the last time we did so when we weren't preparing a lesson. This chapter is an invitation to slow down long enough to figure out what it means to live what we say we believe. This is not an easy task.

In a perfect world, all actions would be intentional and reflective of the will of God. The world in which we live and breathe, however, is not perfect; much "ministry" occurs apart from the truths handed down through disciplines over the centuries. Miroslav Volf offers a succinct response to this concern.

> Often theologians have done theology as if it were a theoretical science; that . . . has contributed to a sense that theology is unrelated to "real" life. . . . Theology is an (academic) enterprise whose object of study is God and God's relation to the world and whose purpose is not simply to deliver "knowledge," but to serve a way of life.[1]

The relationship between theology and practical theology is like that between a medical researcher and practitioner. Researchers would be unable to have the depth of research if, they were seeing patients; doctors would be unable to see patients if they spent all of their time in research. The researcher and doctor need one another to better treat patients. Doctors meet with patients and consider how their prior knowledge and experience intersects with the new information coming from their patients; researchers hear reports from doctors about their interactions with patients, and such feedback informs their ongoing search for new knowledge. If, however, there was never any dialogue between the two, the researchers run the risk of becoming irrelevant and the doctor obsolete. Practical theology similarly opens dialogue to consider the intersection of the theological in everyday life—"reflecting critically upon, learning from, and endeavoring to renew, reform and strengthen practice and, in particular, Christian practice."[2]

---

[1]Miroslav Volf and Dorothy Bass, eds., *Practicing Theology: Beliefs and Practices in Christian Life* (Grand Rapids: Eerdmans, 2002), pp. 246-47.

[2]Duncan Forrester, *Theological Fragments: Explorations in Unsystematic Theology* (New York: T & T Clark, 2005), p. 53.

THE SPIRITUAL QUALITY OF PEOPLE

Adolescence is the perfect place to consider the spiritual quality of human existence; in particular, the relationship of the spirit and soul. While this is not the exclusive domain of adolescence, it is in adolescence where one first recognizes an existential otherness. We may understand humanity by thinking of a Mobius strip, a continuous loop with the soul on one side and the spirit on the other, in a similar way to how Jesus is both fully human and fully divine.

Understandings of the spirit and soul are complex, but there is precedence and evidence for their distinctions and relations.[3] Within quantum and postmodern physics, for example, is the notion of the logic of complementarity, defined by quantum physicist Niels Bohr as "the logical relation between two descriptions or sets of concepts which, though mutually exclusive, are nevertheless both necessary for an exhaustive description of the situation."[4] James Loder describes the model as

> an asymmetrical bipolar relationality in which there is reciprocity between polarity and polarity. . . . The Mobius band at the center illustrates the counterintuitive fact that, although it appears that two distinct polarities are being related, they are, in a more subtle and profound sense, a unity.[5]

The spiritual quality of human existence is found in the relationship between the spirit and soul. Distinctions of spirit and soul may be found in Hebrews 4:12-13 (NRSV):

---

[3]There is no consensus on the understanding of spirit and soul. For further discussions see Warren S. Brown, Nancey Murphy and H. Newton Maloney, eds., *Whatever Happened to the Soul? Scientific and Theological Portraits of Human Nature* (Minneapolis: Augsburg Fortress, 1998); Nancey Murphy, Iain Torrance et al., eds., *Bodies and Souls, or Spirited Bodies* (New York: Cambridge University Press, 2006).

[4]Max Jammer, *The Conceptual Development of Quantum Mechanics* (New York: McGraw Hill, 1966), p. 348. Russell Haitch also refers to quantum physics as a way to wrestle with humanity: Russell Haitch, "Trampling Down Death by Death," in *Redemptive Transformation in Practical Theology: Essays in Honor of James Loder,* ed. Dana Wright and John Kuentzel (Grand Rapids: Eerdmans, 2004), p. 48.

[5]James Loder, "Incisions from a Two-Edged Sword," in *The Treasure of Earthen Vessels: Explorations in Theological Anthropology, in Honor of James N. Lapsley* (Louisville, Ky.: Westminster John Knox, 1994), p. 155.

Indeed, the word of God is living and active, sharper than any two-edged sword, piercing until it divides soul from spirit, joints from marrow; it is able to judge the thoughts and intentions of the heart. And before him no creature is hidden, but all are naked and laid bare to the eyes of the one to whom we must render an account.

According to Loder's model, the human spirit is in relation with the Holy Spirit; the soul is in relation with Jesus' humanity. While Jesus is without sin, we in our humanity are not. It is the soul, then, which is in need of transformation.

Loder agrees with Wolfhart Pannenberg in his understanding of the spirit as "not hidden within the soul but hidden by its very transcendence with respect to it."[6] The soul becomes a frame of reference for the spirit—mutually exclusive, yet necessarily linked: "Within any frame of reference, when new previously hidden orders of meaning emerge to alter the basic axioms of that frame of reference, transformation has taken place."[7]

When the spirit is addressed apart from the soul, ministry becomes a litmus test of behaviors and morals denying the need for actual transformation. Thomas Moore perceives that "when spirituality loses its soul it takes on the shadow-form of fundamentalism."[8] Herbert Anderson calls for a restoration of the soul, believing that it

> will enhance the recovery of paradox in the human life. The soul coming from God, participates fully in its salvation even while it waits for the Lord. Insisting on the soul's paradox will not eliminate dualistic impulses or modify absolutizing tendencies. It will however articulate an anthropological vision that is deep enough and broad enough to encompass the diversity of human life today.[9]

So, in youth ministry as in all ministry, we are to care for the whole person.

---

[6]Ibid., p. 158.

[7]Ibid., p. 166.

[8]Thomas Moore, *Care of the Soul: A Guide for Cultivating Depth and Sacredness in Everyday Life* (New York: HarperCollins, 1992), p. 234.

[9]Herbert Anderson, "The Recovery of Soul," in *The Treasure of Earthen Vessels: Explorations in Theological Anthropology*, ed. Brian Childs and David Waanders (Louisville, Ky.: Westminster John Knox, 1994), p. 221.

CHRIST AT THE CENTER

A distinctly Christocentric approach to practical theology "believes that realities need to be transformed, transfigured, revolutionized, converted, transfigured. . . . This transformation is not a matter of human effort alone, or something to be awaited passively, or effected by a change of understanding alone."[10] As youth workers, we are called to *intentionality*—actively seeking to join God's work in maturing adolescents, in which love, justice and mercy unite to nurture them (individually, communally and eternally) through the transformative power of Christ.

For Daniel Migliore, faith is "no sedative" but rather "incites reflection, inquiry, and pursuit of the truth not yet possessed, or only partially possessed."[11] Migliore goes further to remind us that "believers do not live in a vacuum. Like all people, they live in particular historical situations that have their own distinctive problems and possibilities."[12] Throughout history God has met human persons in the concrete situations of their lives and in doing so responds to the very real issues that confront them. God is embedded in history because we exist in history, the reality of time and space. So practical theology that is Christocentric "strives to engage with questions of truth in relation to practice in general, Christian practice and ministerial practice."[13] This is a concept well expressed by Dietrich Bonhoeffer: "The Body of Christ takes up space on earth. That is a consequence of the Incarnation. Christ came into his own. But at his birth they gave him a manger. . . . At his death they thrust him out, and his Body hung between earth and heaven on the gallows. But despite all this, the Incarnation does involve a claim to a space of its own on earth."[14]

As Gustavo Gutierrez suggests, it is out of the real struggles for freedom and justice and situations in life that the questions for theology

---

[10]Forrester, *Theological Fragments*, p. 27.

[11]Daniel Migliore, *Faith Seeking Understanding: An Introduction to Christian Theology* (Grand Rapids: Eerdmans, 2004), p. 3.

[12]Ibid., p. 4.

[13]Forrester, *Theological Fragments*, p. 55.

[14]Dietrich Bonhoeffer, *The Cost of Discipleship* (New York: Touchstone, 1995), pp. 248-49.

arise.[15] While the practical effect does need to come from a doctrinal truth,[16] the questions that drive us to seek out a doctrine come from the world in which we live. Youth ministry, by its very nature, looks at the current struggles in the lives of teens with whom the youth minister lives, works and serves. One's beliefs impact practice *and* one's practice impacts one's beliefs; they are indeed in conversation, and like any conversation, each participant is impacted. Each, however, retains its own selfhood, not collapsing into an unrecognizable third. A thoughtful and reflective consideration balances the truths that emanate from both doctrinal understandings and the insights of other disciplines, something Paul Tillich calls the "method of correlation" between existential questions and theology:

> Question and answer are independent of each other, since it is impossible to derive the answer from the question or the question from the answer. The existential question, namely, man himself in the conflicts of his existential situation, is not the source for the revelatory answer formulated by theology. One cannot derive the divine self-manifestation from an analysis of the human predicament. . . . Man cannot receive an answer to a question he has not asked.[17]

God is calling us to seek deeper understandings, driven by the concrete situations of our lives and constantly reflecting upon him in our fragmented world. It is important to note that while a person may not be able to receive (or at least recognize what she has received) prior to the question being asked, this is precisely the task of theology. As situations occur, the question is formed, and as faith seeks understanding, theology speaks into the life of the situation in

---

[15]Gustavo Gutierrez, *Essential Writings*, ed. James B. Nickoloff (Maryknoll, N.Y.: Orbis, 1996), pp. 33-34.

[16]"The practical effect or application of a doctrine is a consequence of the truth of the doctrine, not the reverse." Millard Erickson, *Christian Theology* (Grand Rapids: Baker, 1991), p. 22.

[17]Paul Tillich, *Systematic Theology* (Chicago: University of Chicago Press, 1967), 2:13. While not a direct correlation, Immanuel Kant conceptually discussed such matters; see *Groundwork of the Metaphysics of Morals*, trans. H. J. Paton (San Francisco: Harper Torchbooks, 1956).

a new way particular to that point in history.

Correlation is only one methodology among many.[18] It indeed has criticisms, including the assumption that "instead of mutual enhancement, over time, each discipline seeks to subordinate the other."[19] There is also a concern that over time the correlations will tend to unravel and that cultural issues will become problematic in the dialogue.[20] Of course, there is potential for any dialogue to unravel over time. Knowing that this is a possibility if not a probability, intentionality in communication maintains open dialogue. The same is true regarding cultural issues. Where there is a commitment to open dialogue with a great awareness of the struggles to come, space is created for the hard work to follow. Keeping these potential struggles at the forefront of thought, they can become strengths. As with all dialogue, shifts over time require many of the same conversations to be revisited and updated. This is the reality of a dynamic world seeking understanding.

YOUTH MINISTRY AS THEOLOGICAL CONTEXT

The increased interest in practical theology has been accompanied by three major changes in society. First, Christianity is no longer the normative force in contemporary society. Second, as the social sciences continue to rise in use, new vocabularies and methods must be developed and learned to aide interdisciplinary dialogue. Finally, as Charles Scalise has observed, a contextualization of theology has been taking place.[21] Youth ministry is one of these contexts.

---

[18]Charles Scalise offers a clear look at four other methodological approaches to practical theology: contextual, narrative, performance and regulative. Charles Scalise, *Bridging the Gap: Connecting What You Learned in Seminary with What You Find in the Congregation* (Nashville: Abingdon, 2003). While vestiges of each approach can be recognized throughout this book, the connection with the contextual approach is clear in that my ultimate focus is adolescence. Also clearly evident is the narrative approach; my time with Jim McClendon left a lasting impression on my thinking.

[19]Ibid., p. 58.

[20]Ibid., pp. 59-60.

[21]Ibid., pp. 66-88. See also Paul Ballard and John Pritchard, *Practical Theology in Action: Christian Thinking in the Service of Church and Society* (London: SPCK, 1996), pp. 1-5.

Contextualized theology has two particular implications: first, theological work in each context requires its own tasks, interests and methods; second, all theology is to be seen by the normative of the practical—neither theology nor action is mutually exclusive. Taking all of this into account, "practical theology therefore is the place where the reality of all theology as a practical discipline is clearly manifest."[22]

COMMON TERMS IN PRACTICAL THEOLOGY

Before looking at a few key contributors and my chosen methodology, it will be helpful to define a few commonly used terms. For all practical theological writings the distinction between *practice* and *praxis* is important. Practice is the action that follows from theory. Theory was learned from biblical and doctrinal understandings and applied to action, primarily within the church. It was a one-way lecture from the traditional biblical hermeneutic as absolute applied to circumstance.[23] Duncan Forrester offers a clear distinction between practice and praxis:

> When the term "praxis" is preferred to "practice," the emphasis is on the reflective or meaning content of behaviour, the integral interaction between theory and practice. Praxis usually refers to transformative practice.[24]

Praxis is more than practice.[25] It recognizes that no action is value-free but rather requires an analytical critique, including examining

---

[22]Ballard and Pritchard, *Practical Theology in Action*, pp. 1-5.

[23]While practical theology has moved far beyond this position, it is the foundation. At the time, it was a calling back to the church to be intentional about its role, for doctrine to impact what the clergy was doing and shed light on the discrepancy between what is and what ought to be. Schleiermacher is often cited as the father of modern practical theology for bringing attention to this issue.

[24]Forrester, *Theological Fragments*, p. 7.

[25]In many fields *praxis* has become a buzzword. While this is helpful, in some senses moving from an anxiety to be "doing" without any thought, the use of the word seems to lend a sense of credibility, but each user defines it in such differing ways with little consideration to the nuances present that it makes for a confusing conversation. Its origins reside long ago with Aristotle.

one's own presuppositions and biases. It is a hermeneutical dialogue between practice to theory and back to practice (or vice versa).

Critical reflection is not as simple as it seems. The connection of belief with practice can be clouded by the subjective nature intrinsic in the development of praxis. Amy Plantinga Pauw recognizes this reality: "Desires and dispositions play a key role in connecting beliefs and practices."[26] While one may wish to be completely objective, the very nature of reflection itself makes it subjective to the one reflecting.

This applies to language as well. Even the most basic of words may need to be parsed for clarification. Clifford Geertz offers the notion of *thick description* to differentiate between words and terms.[27] Words are simply a combination of letters in a certain order that often carry many meanings. A term moves beyond this and is "defined as an unambiguous word" or "a word used unambiguously."[28] Language is used to communicate, address, support or transform a situation. Thick description takes into account the rich texture of perspectives that permeate and surround issues, questions or observations, ultimately arriving at a fuller connection.[29]

Even a seemingly simple word (for example, *mom*), though it is often used thinly, carries with it a vast amount of thick meaning. *Mom,* meaning the biological woman who birthed or helped to raise a child into adulthood, is thickly described in a variety of ways. For some this conjures up warm thoughts, security, the memory of cookies baking and laughter. For others, *mom* is a harsh or feared word, evoking respect but not love. For even others still, *mom* has nothing to do with biology but a (typically) female elder who has taken a nurturing role at some point in their life. It is nearly impossible to offer a generic statement about *mom* that would be applicable in every situation. The need for an awareness of

---

[26]Volf and Bass, *Practicing Theology,* p. 34.

[27]Clifford Geertz, *The Interpretation of Cultures* (New York: Basic, 1973). Geertz spends the entirety of the first section of this book unpacking the term "thick description."

[28]Mortimer Adler and Charles Van Doren, *How to Read a Book: The Classic Guide to Intelligent Reading* (New York: Touchstone, 1972), pp. 96-97.

[29]Don S. Browning, *A Fundamental Practical Theology: Descriptive and Strategic Proposals* (Minneapolis: Fortress, 1996), pp. 16-17, 58.

thickness in meaning is essential.[30] The hard work comes in not simply reflecting as an individual and assuming it to be true but to reflect considering one's embedded issues and to seek reflection in community, which leads to a greater understanding and ultimately the next term.

This is similar to the concept of *embedded theology*,[31] what is stated directly and indirectly within a community of believers. It is often the most difficult of theologies to discuss, as it is hardly considered a theology at all; it simply is what is, within that church and that culture. While there are points of commonality, not all people share the same embedded theology, which highlights the need to tease out what is meant by a word or phrase. While Stone and Duke distinguish "embedded theology" from "deliberate theology," thick description provides a bridge between the two.

To go after the thickness of meaning requires the hard work of clearly communicating what is intended and what is received in a dialogue. It is concerned with context, taking otherwise ambiguous concepts seeking concretization unambiguously.

At the turn of the twentieth century, philosopher and psychologist William James was openly and publicly concerned with experience allowing one to see more clearly; action was what illuminated ultimate truth. Congregational minister and hospital chaplain Anton Boisen, a follower of James, saw both the patient and chaplain as learners from crisis about not only the presenting crisis but also themselves and their own beliefs. Around 1950 Seward Hiltner, following in this same tradition, established the Religion and Personality program at the University of Chicago. Two major contributions came to American clinical pastoral education from this program: (a) theoretical knowledge equally is developed out of and contributes to practice; (b) the individual is actually participating in the process. "This is based on three assumptions:

---

[30]The debate concerning language within the academy is no less prevalent today than in the past. With the increase in specialization, it is even more of an issue. There are several excellent articles addressing this topic including Chris Barrigar, " 'Thick' Christian Discourse in the Academy: A Case Study with Jürgen Habermas," *Christian Scholar's Review* 34, no. 3 (Spring 2005).

[31]Howard H. Stone and James O. Duke, *How to Think Theologically* (Minneapolis: Fortress, 1996), pp. 12-16.

(1) the way one cares for others is inescapably related to the way one cares for oneself; (2) pastoral caring always involves *being* someone as well as *doing* something; and (3) one can best learn about oneself and how to care for others through experiential and reflective participation in caring relationships."[32]

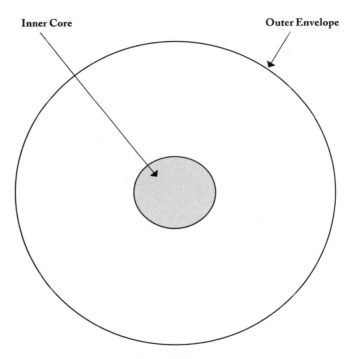

Inner Core   **Outer Envelope**

Diagram 1. Don Browning, *A Fundamental Practical Theology.* **The outer envelope is the well of personal narratives, inherited narratives and practices that tradition has handed to us surrounding our practical thinking. The inner core is at the heart of the narrative and determines the understanding of practical reason.**

Don Browning was a student of Seward Hiltner in the University of Chicago program. While he has edited or contributed to a number of works, his *A Fundamental Practical Theology: Descriptive and Strategic Proposals* is his definitive work to date. What is typically labeled as Brown-

---

[32]James Woodward and Stephen Pattison, eds., *The Blackwell Reader in Pastoral and Practical Theology* (Oxford: Blackwell, 2000), p. 53.

ing's view of practical theology is actually his understanding of theology as a whole: four submovements of descriptive, historical, systematic and strategic theologies.[33] He uses a narrative approach and wishes for all theology to be practical through the narrative to its very heart.

It is this understanding of narrative (what Browning calls the outer envelope) and that which is at the heart of the narrative (what Browning calls the inner core) that determines his understanding of practical reason (see diagram 1).[34] The outer envelope is filled with tradition-saturated (thick) narratives, practices and images of the way the world is according to our experiences.[35] "The envelope of practical reason is the focus of that larger task of reconstructing our experience by reconstructing, amending, or reconsolidating our more general picture of the world."[36] That which is at the heart of the narrative is the inner core and determines the understanding of practical reason. The understanding of the inner core is shaped by tradition but needs the outer envelope to have a sense of the wider world in which it exists. It is ultimately God's story which holds all of this together.

The inner core is what, to me, makes Browning's approach appealing. Practical reason always has a narrative envelope, Browning avers, but it is not necessarily Christian. This allows for dialogue with other concrete narratives, whether they are religiously implicit, explicit or void. (It also opens the possibility for seriously misunderstanding where Browning himself stands as a Christian.) While it does open a path for dialogue, Browning's distinctly Christian perspective is not intended as an apologetic, but rather as a systematic approach to theology in everyday life.

> The inner core functions within a narrative about God's creation, governance, and redemption of the world. It is that fundamental truth within the narrative that includes creation, redemption and the incarnation. It also functions within a narrative that tells how the life and death of Jesus Christ further God's plan for the world.

---

[33]Browning, *Fundamental Practical Theology*, p. 8.
[34]Ibid., pp. 11, 40.
[35]Ibid., p. 11.
[36]Ibid., p. 40.

This (plan) narrative is the outer envelope of practical reason.[37]

The death, burial and resurrection of Jesus is the inner core; it is the heart of the narrative. The outer envelope is God's ultimate plan.

REFLEXIVE CONSIDERATION

Practical reason had traditionally been an individual exercise. Browning applies this same concept to a community as it thinks through practically the circumstances it faces. While there is always a risk of manipulating theory to the need and to the thick understandings of the individual or group, there is something artificial and unrealistic in clinging to the idea that actions can be determined solely by theory. A community, for example, may be committed to giving each person a chance until they have proven to be untrustworthy. This sounds noble until a child molester asks to care for third graders unsupervised. The context must influence the understanding of the theory and lead to an altered practice. While this is a rather extreme example to make a point, this reflexive consideration is what occurs in an instant for each individual or community whether it is recognized or not.

It is important to understand the relationship between theory and practice. "Theory must constantly be tested in praxis. . . . At the same time, praxis must receive a constant critical review from theory."[38] Ray Anderson states that ministry precedes and produces theology, not the reverse.

> It must immediately be added, however, that ministry is determined and set forth by God's own ministry of revelation and reconciliation in the world, beginning with Israel and culminating in Jesus Christ and the church. . . . The Holy Spirit unites the doing of ministry to the ministry already accomplished in Christ, establishing a reciprocity between dogma and experience that continually discloses disciplines.[39]

---

[37]Ibid., pp. 11, 40.
[38]Gerben Heitink, *Practical Theology: History, Theory, Action Domains* (Grand Rapids: Eerdmans, 1993), p. 152.
[39]Ray Anderson, *The Shape of Practical Theology* (Downers Grove, Ill.: InterVarsity

Browning uses two questions to focus his use of practical reason: (1) What should we do? And (2) How should we live?[40] This "tradition of practical reason or practical wisdom has its origins in Aristotle's concept of phronesis. Jesus used the word phronesis in the Sermon on the Mount (Matt. 7:24) to refer to the 'wise' persons who listen to the message of Jesus and build their lives upon it."[41] Practical theology offers the lens through which every situation in life may be approached.

Anderson offers that "God's initial act, and every subsequent act of revelation, is a ministry of reconciliation" that sets the pattern for the people of God.[42] "The practice of ministry, then, is not only the appropriate context for doing theological thinking, it is itself intrinsically a theological activity."[43] Not every action, however, is automatically a practice of ministry or theological activity. It is possible to do ministerial actions like a midweek service, discipleship program or mission trip without considering the doctrinal mandates or seeking theological activity as it emerges from divine revelation.[44] Action that is theological therefore must intentionally be in line with God's ministry of reconciliation. Taking this position, I adapt Browning's two questions into one: *How do I best allow God to work through me to bring about reconciliation?* Or, for the purposes of this book, *How do I best allow God to work through me to bring about reconciliation in the lives and world of adolescents?*

TELOS AND AN EXPLICITLY TRINITARIAN APPROACH

The Trinity is fully present in practical theology. Anderson places God the Father around the model, the Holy Spirit as the mediating presence and Christ at the inner core (see diagram 2).[45] I borrow Anderson's

---

Press, 2001), pp. 62-63.

[40]Browning, *Fundamental Practical Theology*, p. 10.

[41]Ibid.

[42]Anderson, *Shape of Practical Theology*, p. 62.

[43]Ibid.

[44]This is the nuance Anderson makes when discussing *poiesis* as being an act where something is made, lacking in *telos*, and praxis as being an act which includes *telos*. Ibid., pp. 49, 54.

[45]Browning himself considers "self-sacrificial love the Christic moment—the moment of grace that helps the ethic of equal regard renew itself. Even though Christ has

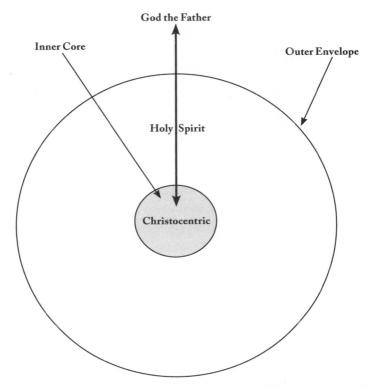

Diagram 2. Ray Anderson's modification of Don Browning's model, as presented in *The Shape of Practical Theology*, making Browning's trinitarian approach more explicit. The Christic moment comes with the inner core, determining the meaning and being an essential element. The Holy Spirit is active throughout, present in the entire experience at work in our individual and communal lives. God the Father is sovereign providing the encompassing narrative.

schema but for slightly different reasons. What Anderson makes explicit is already present in Browning's model. Reconciliation *is* the praxis of God. God does not just do things in the world. His work contains *telos*; every action moves toward this *telos*. This ministry has been present since the Fall, though Jesus ushered in a new paradigm that was completed in the coming of the Holy Spirit. Christ is at the core (the instrument of reconciliation) with the Father providing the outer envelope (whose con-

ethical meaning, I don't reduce my Christology to ethics. . . . It is true: I do not use Christological language to trump all other language games, but I think there is a Christology in the book." Excerpt from an e-mail to the author, dated January 27, 2003.

necting story is that of reconciliation) and the Holy Spirit working through people enabling reconciliation to fulfill this scenario. Just as God came in the incarnation, the Holy Spirit through people provides incarnate grace to bring about reconciliation.[46]

"The Bible speaks of a God who acts, creating, sustaining and redeeming, a God who gives the law to God's people and enjoins them to be perfect as God is perfect—and that involves acting in the style or manner that God acts."[47] It is through the life, the actions and teachings of Jesus that the very actions of God are revealed. Christ, God incarnate, is the greatest example of the life we are to model in following God. Jesus' actions were saturated with intent and belief. Martin Luther's theology of the cross reminds us that "the concept of practice must be broadened to include passion, in both its senses as suffering and emotion."[48] The gospel—offered to humans by God, often through the witness of other humans—is not merely communication of facts; it demands interaction and transformation by its very nature. It seeks to create something new and to surpass human boundaries. It is only through the Holy Spirit that this action is currently possible.

Christocentric praxis takes the action of Christ and presents it in a way that is both christological and christopractical—theologically sound in Christology and based on the actions of Christ.[49] The dialogue is complete, balancing reflection and transformative action. As God's ministry in the world is reconciliation, "human history is the locus of God's activity in time and this always is the first source of God's self-disclosure at any time."[50] The whole Hebrew or Christian

---

[46]Karl Barth offers a much more extensive handling of this subject matter. It is the work of Barth that has also had an impact on Ray Anderson. See Karl Barth, *Church Dogmatics*, trans. G. W. Bromiley, 2nd ed. (Edinburgh: T & T Clark, 1975).

[47]Forrester, *Theological Fragments*, p. 8.

[48]Friedrich Schweitzer and Johannes A. van der Ven, eds., *Practical Theology: International Perspectives* (New York: Peter Lang, 1999), pp. 17-18.

[49]Edmund Arens, *Christopraxis, A Theology of Action* (Minneapolis: Fortress, 1995), p. 90.

[50]Thomas Groome, "Theology on Our Feet: A Revisionist Pedagogy for Healing the Gap Between Academia and Ecclesia," in *Formation and Reflection: The Promise of Practical Theology*, ed. Lewis Mudge and James Poling (Philadelphia: Fortress, 1987), p. 61.

dispensations insist that our God is a God present within history, a God who pitches God's tent and dwells among us (see Leviticus 26:11-13; John 1:14). Unlike the Removed and Unmoved Mover of Greek philosophy, the God of Abraham and Sarah, Moses and Miriam, Jesus and Mary, is indeed God of the heavens but is also God of the earth, an incarnate God who enters into human history with saving power.[51]

Theology begins not in the church, not in a seminary nor college and not with the professional clergy. Theology begins with an understanding that God is already present in daily life. We come to understand this as we tell our narratives, large and small, that make us who we are. We need not seek to understand him in the abstract and hope our dogma fits every situation and circumstance. Our theology emerges from these stories as God reveals himself.

CORRELATION

An abandonment of the traditional disciplines of systematic, historical or biblical theology is not what I am proposing. Rather, I'm seeking a recovery and examination of praxis, both historically and presently, in correlation with the traditional disciplines. Tillich gives an approach to this struggle in *correlation*.[52] Humanity provides the question; God provides the answer. Both are needed for a relationship to exist. This is not to imply that God needs humanity to exist, rather that God needs humanity in order for a relationship to exist between God and humanity.

> If theology gives the answer, "the Christ," to the question implied in human estrangement, it does so differently, depending on whether the reference is to the existential conflicts of Jewish legalism, to the existential despair of Greek skepticism, or to the threat of nihilism as expressed in twentieth-century literature, art, and psychology. Nevertheless, the question does not create the answer. The answer, "the Christ," cannot be created by man, but man can

---

[51]Ibid.
[52]Paul Tillich, *Systematic Theology* (Chicago: University of Chicago Press, 1951), 1:59-65; and Paul Tillich, *Systematic Theology* (Chicago: University of Chicago Press, 1957), 2:13-16.

receive it and express it according to the way he has asked for it.[53]

Our narratives are studied and interpreted by secular disciplines both in social sciences and hard sciences, in fine arts and popular arts, in cultural studies and ethics. Correlation does not elevate one discipline over and above the other. Theology and the secular disciplines are asymmetrical. Theology is seeking an understanding of God, but we are not to negate the possibility of God's revelation within every other field of study. It is not only the right of Christians to enter into dialogue, it is the responsibility. The answer is provided. To "do theology" today means to determine the question.

Correlation can take on many forms. James Poling and Donald Miller acknowledge at least three types with two axes, for a total of six categories.[54] The two axes are on a continuum, between the church as a definite group trying to be faithful in the world and the church as it tries to be responsible to society. The three types are also on a continuum: *critical scientific* uses a secular discipline as the framework and norms, while tradition (theology) plays a secondary role; *critical correlational* seeks a collaborative dialogue between the Christian tradition (or theology) and the secular discipline; in the *critical confessional* type, Christian tradition is considered normative while cautiously considering the secular sciences and minimizing the influence of norms outside of the Christian tradition.

Three questions are offered as a pivot around which all six categories may be found.

- What is the relation of practical theology to philosophy and science?
- What is the relation of practical theology to the Christian story and tradition?
- What is the relation of practical theology to the Christian church in its ideal and institutional forms?[55]

[53]Tillich, *Systematic Theology*, 2:16.
[54]James N. Poling and Donald E. Miller, *Foundations for a Practical Theology of Ministry* (Nashville: Abingdon, 1985), pp. 31-35.
[55]Ibid., p. 36.

These three questions help determine the place of Christian traditions and beliefs as compared with secular and scientific disciplines. A case may be made for any combination of these types and axes. Each needs the other in some form while in and of itself being quite valid. It frequently will be the predisposition one brings to the task of practical theology that will help determine which category is chosen.

Wolfhart Pannenberg argues that all truth is God's truth and ultimately comes together in God.[56] Holding this to be true, to assume some manner of elevated understanding grounded solely in the traditional ecclesial disciplines allows for an unchecked priority of the church and denies the continual revelation of God. To deny his continual revelation would place his ministry of reconciliation in the past, having been both fulfilled and terminated with Christ resurrected and render the Holy Spirit in the contemporary world little more than a reflection of past glory. Critical correlation takes seriously the possibility of God continuing to reveal himself and looks to human history to formulate the question for which we already have the answer.

Theology is and remains a very human undertaking; it may be a revelation of God, but it in no way conducts any kind of divine status itself. Theological and secular scholars as well as clergy are needed, but only as they serve the interpretation of the community—not as they dictate to the community. The Christian tradition must be interpreted and reinterpreted within the context of community. This gives authority equally to the community as well as to scholars and clergy. God is in hierarchical authority.

YOUTH MINISTRY, THE PASTORAL CYCLE AND PRACTICAL THEOLOGY

It would be great if life were only as simple as Ephesians 5:1: "Therefore be imitators of God as beloved children." To imitate God, however, assumes knowledge of how God would act in any given situation. This is at the heart of practical theology and can be observed in the pastoral cycle.

---

[56]Wolfhart Pannenberg, *Systematic Theology*, trans. Geoffrey Bromiley (Grand Rapids: Eerdmans, 1990), 1:59-60.

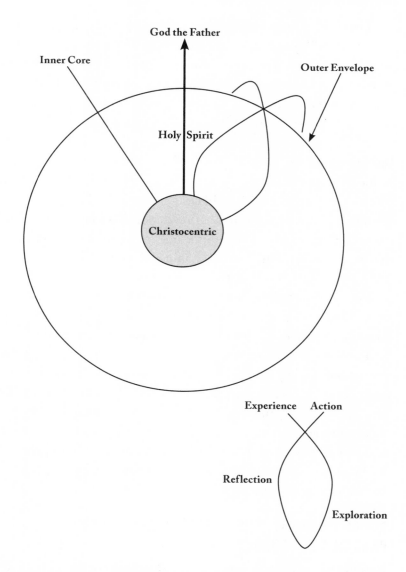

Diagram 3. A trinitarian, Christocentric modification of Browning's fundamental practical theology in union with the pastoral cycle. Every experience or narrative takes place in
the world in which we live. Whether recognized or not, it is connected ultimately to the
encompassing narrative of God. The pastoral cycle allows intentional movement from the
initial experience to the action which follows. An experience is a disruption of the normal
pattern no matter how slight. Exploration takes place as information is gathered seeking
both theological and secular input. Reflection takes seriously what was gathered in the exploration stage, adding critical thinking and tradition as information is considered. Action
is a result of the informed decisions and appropriate initiatives.

The pastoral cycle is a fourfold process: (1) experience, (2) exploration, (3) reflection and (4) action (see diagram 3).[57] *Experience* is the place one begins. This is more than just a random point in time or life. It is the point at which something has disrupted the normal pattern, forcing a change of some manner. It is pregnant with meaning and requiring a thick description. *Exploration* is the information stage—assessing what is happening, gathering information from both a theological perspective and other areas of revelation, discussing, digesting and testing as is relevant to the situation. *Reflection* takes seriously what was learned in the exploration stage but adds to it the reality that individuals do not live in a vacuum. It accounts for personal and communal beliefs—traditions and denominational backdrops—as they correlate. It involves discovery and change. *Action*, the last stage in the cycle, comes from the whole process and is based on reflection, informed decisions and appropriate initiatives. It is what takes place after information has been gathered and the understandings of the community, theological tradition and individual have been considered.

This completes one rotation of the cycle. It is, however, a cycle. As the cycle ends, it begins anew with a different experience, no matter how slight the difference may seem (see diagram 4). Often this cycle occurs within a few seconds, though it can take longer as experiences lapse and as gathering and reflection require varying amounts of time.[58]

Each cycle provides its own story, a new narrative finding its place within the connecting narrative. Whether the concern is the best way to teach students, to meet the needs of a high school girl, to bring change to society or to settle situations in everyday life, imitating God takes intentional effort. As each experience passes, it leaves its imprint as embedded information for future exploration. The experiences may fade with time but they become a layer of an ever increasing web of life (see diagram 5).

---

[57]A similar and accepted alternative is used by Richard Osmer looking to four major tasks: (1) the descriptive-empirical, (2) the interpretive, (3) the normative and (4) the pragmatic. Richard Robert Osmer, *The Teaching Ministry of Congregations* (Louisville, Ky.: Westminster John Knox, 2005), p. xv.

[58]Ibid., pp. 77-78.

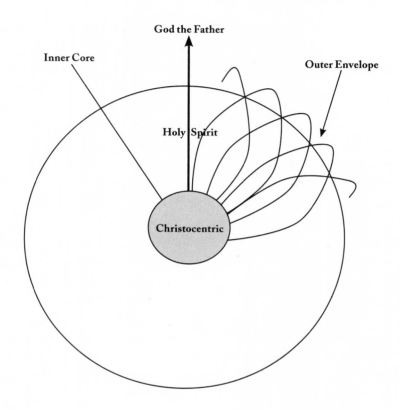

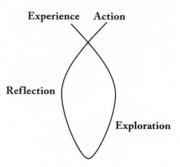

Diagram 4. The pastoral cycle begins anew with each different experience, no matter how slight. It may occur literally in the space of a few seconds from one another or cover a much greater amount of time. The amount of information needed to be gathered and reflection required will vary greatly based on the experience. Each experience or narrative fits into the encompassing narrative of the sovereignty of God.

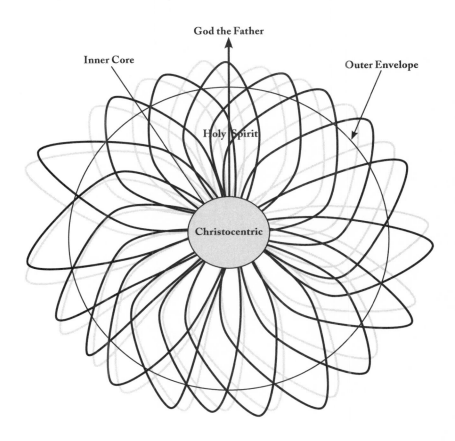

Diagram 5. As each cycle occurs, what is imbibed is not left behind. With each experience, adjustments are made and transformation takes place. Each cycle provides its own story, a new narrative finding its place within the encompassing narrative. While past events do not necessarily play a prominent role in one's life as time passes, the echoes of transformation will linger, tying event to event throughout one's life.

Youth ministry offers not only a constant stream of narratives but narratives that span the range from very mundane to life-threatening. The role of the youth worker is not simply to act (understanding that an action may intentionally be listening, not necessarily "action" as in needing to intervene) but to act phronetically with an intent of finding the best way for God to work through me to bring about reconciliation in the life of the student, regardless of what this may mean. When done properly, practical theology ensures that the youth worker considers the theological implications and ramifications within a given situation.

QUESTIONS FOR FURTHER THOUGHT

1. What do you find that most keeps you from reflective thought?

2. How has the youth ministry that you do already affirmed the bilingual conversation, addressing both the human needs and spiritual needs of teenagers?

3. What do you think the relation between theology and ministry should be?

4. How might your youth group employ the pastoral cycle and practical theology to live out what they say they believe?

3

OVERLAPPING SPHERES IN ADOLESCENT DEVELOPMENT

HEALTHY INDIVIDUATION

There is something at work in my soul which I do not understand.

MARY SHELLEY, *FRANKENSTEIN*

To be rooted is perhaps the most important and least recognized need of the human soul.

SIMONE WEIL

Don't let anyone make you their slogan, remember that you are poetry.

GWEN, *28 DAYS*

I LED A PARENT WORKSHOP A few months ago at a local church. I wasn't sharing any secret information, not even information that was all that profound—to me, at least. We were simply talking about adolescent development: what is really occurring, what has shifted over the years and what is "normal." I forget not everyone knows this stuff.

That particular workshop I had parents crying, others expressing relief and all raising a flood of questions that ended in a beautiful conversation between the parents.

Teenagers can be frustrating. After years of working with teens, we can forget that each new group is a new group *of teens;* it's we, not they, who have gotten older. Teens are supposed to experiment with roles. They will be unpredictable. They will have a roller coaster of emotions. They will have highs and lows as they try to discover themselves. While longing to become their own individual person, they will look to do so in groups. They will grow up. We have been blessed to walk with them for a short season of their lives, but what a season it is!

The most common area of complaint I get from students is in having to study adolescent development and not just get on to the business of ministry. And yet our time spent on adolescent development is what they express being thankful for a few years into the job. Understanding adolescent development can be one of the greatest tools a youth pastor has to stay in ministry for the long haul.

Teenagers are all about change; consequently, on some level so must be youth ministry. A practical theology of youth ministry requires that we acknowledge and address the changes which occur between childhood and adulthood. I propose a holistic look at adolescent development; one which comprises not only biological and sociological issues but equally pays attention to the spirit.

THE IMPORTANCE OF ADOLESCENT DEVELOPMENT

Why is it important to know adolescent development? Andrea Solarz offers one of the most compelling reasons I have read.

> Today's adolescent needs one thing that adults seem to have the least surplus of—time. It takes time to listen to an adolescent. . . . A crosscutting theme, regardless of one's professional role, is the need to communicate effectively with youth. Adolescents will not simply "open up" to adults on demand. Effective communication requires that an emotional bond form, however briefly, between the professional and the adolescent. For this bond to form, professionals must be knowledgeable about normal adolescent development.[1]

---

[1]Andrea Solarz, *Healthy Adolescents Project: Adolescent Development Project* (Washington, D.C.: American Psychological Association, 2002), p. 4.

Apart from all of the ministerial implications within an incarnational approach to youth ministry, needing to understand adolescent development in order to have effective communication makes the argument that much more persuasive. Duncan Forrester's warning that often we as ministers and theologians are answering questions no one is asking is all too true.

In order for a practical theology of youth ministry to be effective it is important to have a clear and cohesive understanding of adolescence. As adolescence increasingly describes a psychological as well as cultural condition, a solitary definition across disciplines is elusive. Developmental psychologist John Santrock offers a widely acceptable definition of adolescence as "the period of transition between childhood and adulthood that involves biological, cognitive and socioemotional changes."[2]

Adolescence is a relatively new construct. The academic study of it is even more recent, making its formal appearance courtesy of G. Stanley Hall during the span of 1890-1920 and specifically in a textbook published in 1904, where he states that "at no time of life is the love of excitement so strong as during the season of accelerated development of adolescence, which craves strong feelings and new sensations."[3] While the advent of the term *adolescence* for this season of life is only one hundred years old, the concept is evident far back in Western history. As far back as the fourth century B.C., Plato was offering his thoughts on children, teenagers and their capabilities. Plato is known for not believing children were rational, as roughly defined before the age of seventeen. He deferred anything beyond stories and gymnastics till age twenty.

---

[2]John Santrock, *Adolescence*, 11th ed. (New York: McGraw Hill, 2007), p. 17. Adolescence fits into the larger picture of human development. There are many approaches to systematize and understand what occurs along the life cycle. These include but are not limited to social learning theory, information processing theory, psychoanalytic approaches (most notably Freud), humanistic psychology and ethology. The purpose of this chapter is not to offer an exhaustive look at adolescence from every theoretical angle. While being influenced by and employing both cognitive and psychoanalytic approaches, their position within a larger systemic picture will become evident.
[3]G. Stanley Hall, *Adolescence: Its Psychology and Its Relation to Physiology, Anthropology, Sociology, Sex, Crime, Religion, and Education*, vols. 1-2 (Englewood Cliffs, N.J.: Prentice Hall, 1904), p. 368.

It's out of the question for them to do anything else during the period in question, which may last for two or three years, because exertion and exhaustion don't mix with intellectual work. . . . After this period, I went on, a select group of the twenty-year-olds will receive a promotion above the rest, and will be required to consolidate the subjects they were taught unsystematically as children until they gain an overview of the relationships these subjects have to one another and to reality.[4]

Adolescence as it exists today covers a span of roughly fifteen years: early adolescence (approximately age ten to fourteen), middle (approximately age fifteen to eighteen) and late (approximately age seventeen to twenty-five).[5] This is not a new characterization; Peter Blos cites the term "prolonged adolescence" as being introduced by Siegfried Bernfeld as early as 1923.[6] Even further back, Saint Augustine offers a recollection of his late teen and early twenties. "So for the space of nine years (from my nineteenth birthday to my twenty-eighth year) I lived a life in which I was seduced and seducing, deceived and deceiving, the prey of various desires."[7] While not a behavioral norm in his day, for those in privileged, wealthy families like Augustine, this was a reality. What makes "prolonged adolescence" more significant and pervasive today may be a matter of sheer numbers and cultural mainstreaming.[8]

---

[4]Plato, *Republic*, trans. Robin Waterfield (Oxford: Oxford University Press, 1993), pp. 71, 271.

[5]Jeffrey Jensen Arnett, *Adolescence and Emerging Adulthood: A Cultural Approach*, 4th ed. (Upper Saddle River, N.J.: Prentice Hall, 2009), p. 17. Arnett uses the terms *early adolescence*, *late adolescence* and *emerging adulthood*; for consistency I will use *early*, *middle* and *late adolescence*. *Late adolescence* will also be synonymous with *young adulthood*. I will periodically make reference to this construct, but I will most often be discussing adolescence in the broadest perspective.

[6]Peter Blos, *The Adolescent Passage: Developmental Issues* (New York: International University Press, 1979), p. 38.

[7]Augustine, *Confessions*, trans. Rex Warner (New York: Signet Classic, 2001), p. 56.

[8]For further consideration of late adolescence see Scott A Boles, "A Model of Parental Representations, Second Individuation, and Psychological Adjustment in Late Adolescence," *Journal of Clinical Psychology* 5, no. 4 (1999): 497-512.

INDIVIDUATION

The seemingly simplistic task of adolescence is known most often as individuation.[9] Carl Jung offered the first understanding of this concept when referring to the task of those around age thirty as "becoming one's own person," "coming to self" or "self-realization."[10] Margaret Mahler, however, picks up on this term and applies it in a very different way. Most of her work focuses on the mother and the child's first three years of life. Mahler believes an individual begins in a state of psychological fusion with the mother and progresses gradually to separation. The unfinished crises and residues of the earlier state of fusion, as well as the process of separating and individuating, profoundly influence relationships later in life. Mahler assigns the separation/individuation process to the period beginning approximately the fourth or fifth month of life and extending to approximately the thirty-sixth month. During that period the child repeatedly experiences separation from significant others but returns for a sense of confirmation and comfort.[11] It is the job of the parent to teach the infant growing into toddlerhood guidelines for acceptable behavior and coping skills as she is dealing with her dependency needs, both emotional and physical. "The toddlers are torn between a desire to stay close to their mothers and a wish to be independent. Their new sense of freedom seemed to frighten them."[12]

Remove the word *toddler* and anyone who spends any time around adolescents can recognize this description to varying extents as being pertinent. Peter Blos notably introduced this application of individuation to adolescents.[13] This second separation-individuation phase

---

[9]Accepting the term of individuation and acknowledging it is the normative term within the field of youth ministry, I will offer a look at the relevance of psychoanalytic and psychological perspectives for a greater understanding.

[10]Carl Jung, *The Portable Jung*, ed. Joseph Campbell, trans. R. F. C. Hull (New York: Penguin, 1971), p. 121.

[11]Margaret Mahler, "A Study of the Separation and Individuation Process," *The Psychoanalytic Study of the Child* 26 (1971): 403-22.

[12]Grace J. Craig, *Human Development*, 7th ed. (Upper Saddle River, N.J.: Prentice Hall, 1996), p. 237.

[13]Peter Blos proposes "to view adolescence in its totality as the second individuation process, the first one having been completed toward the end of the third year of life." Blos, *Adolescent Passage*, p. 142.

describes the child moving toward adulthood and experiencing "the shedding of family dependencies, the loosening of infantile object ties in order to become a member of society at large or, simply, of the adult world."[14] The child separates not from the family but from the role of child.

> Blos believes it is critical for adolescents to gain difference and distance from parents to transcend infantile ties to them. Individuation during adolescence is defined as a sharpened sense of one's distinctness from others, a heightened awareness of one's self-boundaries . . . individuation in adolescence means that individuals now take increasing responsibility for what they do and what they are, . . . rather than depositing their responsibility on the shoulders of those under whose influence and tutelage they have grown up.[15]

Jung's original understanding helps to set the context for even this modification of his original concept. He believed there was a difference between individuation and individualism.

> Individualism means deliberately stressing and giving prominence to some supposed peculiarity rather than to collective considerations and obligations. But individuation means precisely the better and more complete fulfillment of the collective qualities of the human being, since adequate consideration of the peculiarity of the individual is more conducive to a better social performance than when the peculiarity is neglected or suppressed.[16]

Individuation takes seriously the individual seeking not only how to become one's own self but one's own best self. This is done certainly with attention to the particularity of an individual but equally so for the good that is brought to the social collective. By implication, then, individuation takes into account the greater story, history and the place

---

[14]Ibid.
[15]Santrock, *Adolescence*, p. 226.
[16]Jung, *Portable Jung*, p. 122.

of the individual within the universe and its relation to other individuals.[17] The importance of this will become apparent in further considerations of adolescent development.

ERIKSON AND PIAGET: DEVELOPMENT FORERUNNERS

No survey of development would be adequate without considering the work of Jean Piaget and Erik Erikson. Shifting the perception of "human beings as passive machines acted on by the environment" to "human beings as rational, active, alert and competent,"[18] Piaget, a Swiss psychologist, introduced four stages of mental development: sensorimotor, preoperational, concrete and formal operational. This fourth stage begins at age twelve and extends throughout life. Individuals in this stage are able to investigate logical responses in both concrete and abstract ways, as well as project to the future.[19]

Erik Erikson, a third-generation Freudian, takes this epigenetic approach much further and offers eight stages: hope, will, purpose, competence, fidelity, love, care and wisdom. It is his fifth and sixth stages with which youth ministry may be informed: fidelity (age twelve through eighteen), coinciding roughly with puberty and adolescence, where an individual is seeking identity; and love (age eighteen and over), which coincides with young adulthood and seeks intimacy versus isolation.[20]

In adolescence, the central issue is identity versus identity confusion. The healthy path in adolescence involves establishing a clear and definite sense of who you are and how you fit into the world around you. The unhealthy alternative is identity confusion, a failure to form a stable and secure identity. Identity formation involves sifting through the range of life choices available in your

---

[17]For application within the field of youth ministry see Malan Nel, *Youth Ministry: The Challenge of Individuation* (paper presented at International Association for the Study of Youth Ministry, Oxford, England, January 2003).

[18]Craig, *Human Development*, p. 49.

[19]Jean Piaget, *The Child and Reality: Problems of Genetic Psychology* (New York: Penguin, 1977), pp. 54-61.

[20]Erik Erikson, *The Life Cycle Completed* (New York: W. W. Norton, 1997), pp. 35-36.

culture, trying out various possibilities, and ultimately making commitments.[21]

Identity truly is a huge piece of what it means to individuate. Identity, however, has many aspects and more than one route to achievement. James Marcia has spent a great deal of time on work that springs directly from Erikson's theory. In his view,

> Identity refers to a coherent sense of one's meaning to oneself and to others within that social context. This sense of identity suggests an individual's continuity with the past, a personally meaningful present, and a direction for the future. . . . Within the Eriksonian framework, identity is the expectable outcome of a particular developmental period: adolescence.[22]

Marcia views his responsibility as a psychologist to move beyond theory to that which is both valid and useful. He has formulated four identity statuses that are now widely accepted and referenced within adolescent research: identity achievement, moratorium, foreclosure and identity diffusion.

> Identity achievement persons have undergone significant exploration and have made commitments. . . . Moratorium individuals are currently in the exploratory period; hence, their commitments are not firm, but they are struggling actively to arrive at them. They may be said to be in an identity crisis. The third identity status is Foreclosure. These persons, while strongly committed, have not arrived at their commitments via the route of exploration; they have retained, virtually unquestioned, the values and occupational directions of their childhood. . . . Identity Diffusion comprises the final identity status. These individuals may have undergone some tentative explorations, but this has actually been more like wandering than exploring. The hallmark of the Diffu-

---

[21]Arnett, *Adolescence and Emerging Adulthood*, p. 170.
[22]James Marcia, "The Empirical Study of Ego Identity," in *Identity and Development: An Interdisciplinary Approach*, ed. Harke Bosma, Tobi Graafsma, Harold Grotevant and David deLevita (Thousand Oaks, Calif.: Sage, 1994), pp. 70-71.

sion identity status is a lack of commitment."[23]

The strength of Marcia's position is twofold: its application and its contextualization. Founded on a two-process dimension of exploration and commitment, it alone acknowledges that, while the formation of identity is certainly about the person, it is not done in a vacuum or accomplished in a single point in time; rather, identity formation is a process over a great period of one's life.

Identity is a combination of several layers of identifiers. To focus on secondary roles alone blocks the realization of primary identity which roots and directs the self. Marcia synthesizes the work of two theorists that he sees as "having spoken the most clearly in developmental terms about the self."[24]

> Combining [Mahler and Kohut], perhaps somewhat simplistically, one might say that the self is the outcome of the separation-individuation and rapprochement process undergone by the toddler. This initial self must then be continually responded to and reinforced throughout the lifetime, although the quantity of support needed decreases and the figures qualified to provide it become more selected. Developmentally, the self precedes both the ego ideal and an identity and probably lies the deepest of the three within the personality. A solid sense of self is a necessary, but not a sufficient, condition for identity.[25]

Seth Schwartz wrote a helpful essay calling those who look at development to hearken back to Erikson, because current identity theories neglect the interaction of various aspects.[26] Identity theory must take into account the integration of the individual and social. Using this same concern, I argue that we must consider the eternal dimensions of adolescence.

---

[23]Ibid., p. 73.

[24]Ibid., p. 72.

[25]Ibid.

[26]Seth Schwartz, "A New Identity for Identity Research: Recommendations for Expanding and Refocusing Identity Literature," *Journal of Adolescent Research* 20, no. 3 (May 2005): 296.

The realization of our primary root identification is found deeper than a sense of solid self. It is found in our relationship to God occurring in reconciliation with Christ. David Ford calls it "a new location of self, most succinctly summed up as being 'in Christ.'"[27] "The remaining life process of differentiation is now rooted not in fleeing from but in moving toward origination—a tension between radical individuation and the distinct identity within the communal relationship with Christ. Katherine Turpin is particularly attuned to the communal relationship, both for better and for worse, regarding identity formation. In particular, she takes a detailed look at the modern community built around consumerism and its impact on our vocational choices, and ultimately that which we hold as meaning-making elements in our world. Her concern centers on her belief that "everyone from infants to elders in our society is strongly influenced by the formation of consumer culture"[28] as they miss being formed by "a life of love in the image of Christ."[29] Once again, there is a call back to reconciliation with God and the identity which is ours in Christ.

There are many in the world who have a solid sense of self which poses as their identity. This has much more to do, however, with the "what" of a person than with the "who." The "what" is composed of the actions a person undertakes. Of course, these are not so cleanly separated that the what does not flow out of the who, but it is possible (and in fact probable) that a person's doings ultimately refuse to cede the deeper level of identification.[30] Psychologist Ruthellen Josselson expresses this succinctly: "Our identity theory tended to expand in the direction of doing, of agency, of self-assertion and self-awareness, of mastery, values, and abstract commitment."[31]

---

[27]David Ford, *Self and Salvation: Being Transformed* (New York: Cambridge University Press, 1999), p. 117.

[28]Katherine Turpin, *Branded: Adolescents Converting from Consumer Faith* (Cleveland: Pilgrim Press, 2006), p. 3.

[29]Ibid., p. 7.

[30]Calenthia Dowdy, Pamela Erwin and Amy Jacober, "A New Eden Identity," *Journal of Youth and Theology* (2010).

[31]Ruthellen Josselson, "Identity and Relatedness in the Life Cycle," in *Identity and Development: An Interdisciplinary Approach,* ed. Harke Bosma, Tobi Graafsma, Harold Grotevant and David deLevita (Thousand Oaks, Calif.: Sage, 1994), p. 83.

Marcia raises two other important issues relevant for those who work with adolescents. First, identity formation is a lifelong process, not a stage which occurs within a neat framework of time. This does not negate the presence of individuation; rather, it sets it in context within the greater process of differentiation. Second, one's identity is held not solely within the individual but also in who the individual is *within his or her community.* Separation-individuation is, then, in some senses a misnomer; there is a distancing, a division, that occurs, but the separation is not a complete severance.

Blos's second individuation is the process of turning from the *role of child* to the *role of adult* within community. He describes the second individuation "clinically and theoretically, in terms of progressive development, each marked by a phase-specific conflict, a maturational task, and a resolution that is preconditional for the advance to higher levels of differentiation."[32] This is vastly different from assuming that individuation is completed at a specific point in time for all settings—that separation-individuation amounts to finding one's identity in an isolated, severed individual activity, only to one day return to the community as the newly fashioned adult.

INDIVIDUATION: AN ADOLESCENT STEP IN DIFFERENTIATION

The sense of where one belongs is a significant factor in identity formation, enmeshed as it is with the process of discovering who one is. Josselson acknowledges that adolescents

> undergo a separation-individuation process on the road to identity. But at the same time, they are not becoming "lone selves" needing no one, standing to face the forces of life alone. Rather they are editing and modifying, enriching and extending their connections to others, becoming more fully themselves in relation. Individuation is reinvested in revised relatedness, and in these commitments lies the integration of identity.[33]

We are a communal people. This can be understood from a psycho-

---

[32]Blos, *Adolescent Passage,* p. 141.
[33]Josselson, "Identity and Relatedness," p. 83.

logical or sociological perspective (not to mention a theological perspective): humans simply have, within our nature, the desire not to exist alone. Recent research maintains that "an overemphasis on themes of individual identity, self-reliance, and autonomy as the developmental trajectory of adolescence leads to a lack of attention to the positive, normative mechanisms that permit young adolescents to achieve a sense of belonging and connection."[34]

Kohut, a strong proponent of this sense of connection, "has maintained that people are their healthiest and best when they can feel both independence and attachment. . . . Mature adults feel a basic security grounded in an identity that involves a sense of freedom, self-sufficiency, and self-esteem, they are not compulsively dependent on others, but neither do they have to fear closeness."[35] It is not so much a matter of independent autonomy as it is interdependent autonomy: "Just as the attachment relationship creates a system that serves to protect and promote infant survival, one can argue that . . . subsequent survival depends largely on the ability to form and sustain cooperative, protective groups larger than the immediate family."[36] The process of individuation is less consumed with the independent self; rather, it sets the self within the context of all of creation as interdependent.[37] This is not a particularly Western way of thinking, with our historically extreme emphasis on individualism; yet we too are connected and have always been so.

Kohut's research often has been focused on those who choose (through volitional choice or as a coping mechanism in the face of cir-

[34]Barbara Newman and Philip Newman, "Group Identity and Alienation: Giving the We Its Due," *Journal of Youth and Adolescence* 30 no. 5 (October 2001): 515.
[35]Gerald Corey, *Theory and Practice of Counseling and Psychotherapy*, 4th ed. (Pacific Grove, Calif.: Brooks/Cole, 1991), p. 114.
[36]L. R. Caporael and R. M. Baron, "Groups as the Mind's Natural Environment," in *Evolutionary Social Psychology*, ed. Douglas T. Kenrick and Jeffry A. Simpson (Mahwah, N.J.: Erlbaum, 1997), p. 327.
[37]For further consideration, see Heinz Kohut, *The Search for Self: Selected Writings of Heinz Kohut: 1950-1978*, ed. P. H. Ornstein (New York: International University Press, 1978); and Heinz Kohut, *Self Psychology and the Humanities: Reflections on a New Psychoanalytic Approach*, ed. Charles Strozier (New York: W. W. Norton, 1985).

cumstantial experience) this extreme route of independent individualism, resulting in narcissistic manifestations.[38] Kohut's position asserts that nothing, and consequently no person, exists in and of itself; we are not isolated and independent but rather interdependent and subject to interpretation.[39] Among other issues, Kohut recognizes an "oscillation between states of cohesion and states of disintegration."[40] It is not a linear development as much as it is cyclical with a meandering (but ideally forward) direction. Louise Kaplan notes that as an adolescent advances to adulthood, she will have excursions into her past. "But these excursions are not linear, any more than the forward moves are straight ahead"[41]—at times it amounts to taking two steps forward, one step back; at other times taking one step forward and three steps back. Kohut believes that

> we also learn to understand how during various later developmental stages—including in particular the transition from adolescence to adulthood—it (the self) oscillates, under the impact of internal and external pressures, between renewed fragmentation and regained cohesiveness.[42]

Individuation is a process of moving, in community, toward adulthood—realizing that this movement itself is a piece of the larger, lifelong process of differentiation. This is the reason why thirty-five-year-olds can fall right back into adolescent communication patterns during a holiday visit with family. While no longer an adolescent, the thirty-five-year-old is still working through issues of differentiation.

Each of our theorists recognizes the great importance of the earliest years of development as it influences the second individuation. "With identity formation being considered as less a result of individuation and

---

[38]Corey, *Theory and Practice*, p. 114.

[39]John T. Campbell, "Self or No-Self: Is There a Middle Way?" *Journal of Pastoral Care* 53, no. 1 (1999): 8.

[40]Ibid., p. 9.

[41]Louise J. Kaplan, *Adolescence: The Farewell to Childhood* (New York: Touchstone, 1984), p. 99.

[42]Heinz Kohut, *The Search for the Self*, vol. 2 (New York: International University Press, 1978), p. 579.

more so influenced by attachment relationships with caregivers, researchers have turned to attachment theory as a lens through which to understand adolescent identity development."[43] Attachment theory offers predictors of foundational elements within Kohut's theory of self-cohesion and self-fragmentation.

> Throughout life, individuals strive to maintain a sense of self-cohesion, which refers to experiences of wholeness, stability, and positive self-esteem. In contrast to self-cohesion is self-fragmentation, which may be manifested by anxiety, confusion, emptiness, lethargy, grandiosity, and depression. These feelings, which initially evolve in early childhood experiences, may continue to arise when one is faced with external or internal stresses at any juncture in life.[44]

Individuation does not take place in a vacuum. One needs only look to any seventh grader with whom you have an inside relationship to see the beginnings of what is, at times, seemingly a split personality. He will be a class clown at school, protective older brother in the neighborhood and chief torturer of his little brother at home. He will give a head nod to family in public and fall asleep in a family member's lap on the couch at home, securely hidden from the world. Changes in adolescence appear in every area of life—not merely biology but cognitive,

---

[43]Jessica Samuolis, Kiera Layburn and Kathleen Schiaffina, "Identity Development and Attachment to Parents of College Students," *Journal of Youth and Adolescence* 30, no. 3 (June 2001): 374. The consideration of attachment from birth through the adolescent years could be an entire book. The research is vast and well documented to state that the attachment one experiences early in life will positively or negatively affect development. Attachment toward the mother is strongest in infancy and childhood, the shift (not abandonment) from mother to father occurs in early adolescence, balancing once individuation has taken place and adulthood is reached. It is important for any adult who works with adolescents to have a minimal understanding of issues of attachment and helpful to have a greater understanding. For more consideration of the relationship between parents and emerging adults see Christian Smith and Patricia Snell, *Souls in Transition: The Religious and Spiritual Lives of Emerging Adults* (New York: Oxford University Press, 2009).

[44]David Blustein and Donna Palladino, "Self and Identity in Late Adolescence: A Theoretical and Empirical Integration," *Journal of Adolescent Research* 6, no. 4 (October 1991): 440.

social and spiritual areas as well. Each of these areas influences, and is influenced by, each individual's ever-changing pace of life and growth.

The actual physical changes within adolescence have not changed over the years. What has changed is the timing. Once beginning around age fourteen and ending near age sixteen, adolescence can now begin as early as ten and ends in the mid to late twenties.[45] This reality has been the cause of much discussion and at times alarm. Adults lament that teens are not as mature as they were at that age. It is a cultural shift, however, not a weakness of this generation. We would do well to treat it as such rather than fighting the change.

The fact that adolescents are even thinking *Who am I?* demonstrates one of the most dramatic markers within their journey from childhood to adulthood. While they were children, their thoughts were black and white; object relations were strong. If a child calls a piece of paper a piece of cake in play, it is, for that child, a piece of cake.[46] For an adolescent, however, abstract thoughts, logic, reason and shades of gray enter into their developmental vocabulary. This is not to say that the need for an adult disappears in the life of an adolescent. "Despite stereotypes to the contrary, adolescents prefer to confer with their parents or other trusted adults in making important decisions."[47]

Moral development falls within the realm of cognitive development for an adolescent. Moral development focuses on values and the ethical behavior which proceeds—helping, volunteering, morality, fairness and everyday treatment of others with kindness.[48] Cognitive development looks at the academic side of school and learning as well as the behaviors one chooses, both macro and micro. Social relationships—peer relationships, family, school, work and community—take on an increasingly important position within the life of the adolescent.[49]

---

[45]Arnett, *Adolescence and Emerging Adulthood*, p. 17.

[46]Ibid., p. 52.

[47]Solarz, *Healthy Adolescents Project*, p. 8.

[48]Ibid., p. 11.

[49]For works considering these issues, see the *Journal for Research on Adolescence*, published by the Society for Research on Adolescence; also Chap Clark, *Hurt: Inside the World of Today's Teenagers* (Grand Rapids: Baker Academic, 2004).

Adolescents choose crowds to a certain extent but . . . they also are to some extent assigned to crowds by peers in recognition of their behavioral choices and personalities. . . . Adolescents develop socially construed representations of their peers' identities, or "crowd" identities, which serve not only as pre-existing, symbolic categories through which they can recognize potential friend or foe, tormentor, collaborator, or competitor but also as public identities that are recognized and accepted by peers.[50]

Some have taken the relationship with friends to eclipse the importance of family. Research has shown, however, that "decreased frequency of contact with family does not mean that family closeness has assumed less importance for the adolescent."[51] Rather, this is the realm in which it is most obvious that the process of individuation is occurring.

School, work and community may be seen as the secondary level of significance within the world of an adolescent. School provides socialization and dealings with authority outside of the family experience. "Adolescent perception of teacher fairness has also been found to be associated with positive adolescent development."[52] Work can be both a positive and negative impact on the life of an adolescent. Proper training and supervision provide an adolescent with labor skills and adult, peer and customer interaction; unfortunately, proper training and supervision are rare,[53] and by working the adolescent ends up spending less time with family.[54] The adults involved must take responsibility to make an adolescent's work life a positive con-

---

[50]Bonnie Barber, Jacquelynne Eccles and Margaret Stone, "Whatever Happened to the Jock, the Brain, and the Princess? Young Adult Pathways Linked to Adolescent Activity Involvement and Social Identity," *Journal of Adolescent Research* 16, no. 5 (September 2001): 450, 431.

[51]J. O'Koon, "Attachment to Parents and Peers in Late Adolescence and Their Relationship with Self-Image," *Adolescence* 32 (1997): 472.

[52]M. D. Resnick et al., "Protecting Adolescents from Harm: Findings from the National Longitudinal Study on Adolescent Health," *Journal of the American Medical Association* 278 (1997): 825.

[53]For a rather extreme telling of this, see Eric Schlosser, *Fast Food Nation: The Dark Side of the All-American Meal* (New York: Perennial, 2005), pp. 67-71, 78-87.

[54]Santrock, *Adolescence*, pp. 513-14.

tribution to their developmental process.

Meanwhile, the parent has to capture every moment they can in increasingly limited "shared space."

> The automobile is replacing the kitchen as the gathering place for the family unit. Conversation takes place in the car as it connects the dots of the family's social system, not at the kitchen table.[55]

This may not be the best way to stay in contact as a family, but it is not the child transitioning to adulthood who bears the responsibility.

Community—which includes neighborhoods, schools, clubs, sports, media and religious organizations—can also be a positive or negative factor in adolescent development. The influence is often subtle but pervasive over the years.[56] The institutional church offers a context in which to discuss spiritual development, a process just like every other aspect of the holistic person. Within secular fields is a gracious nod in the direction of God, or a tacit admission that "something out there" has an influence on our lives; adolescents are keenly aware of this and are interested in openly searching and discussing these possibilities. In fact, "the majority of American teenagers appear to espouse rather inclusive, pluralistic, and individualistic views about religious truth, identity boundaries, and need for religious congregations."[57] Much to the chagrin of their parents, "several studies have indicated that deciding on one's own beliefs and values is one of the criteria young people view as most important to becoming an adult."[58] Christian Smith and Melinda Lundquist Denton note, how-

---

[55]Diana Garland, *Family Ministry: A Comprehensive Guide* (Downers Grove, Ill.: Inter-Varsity Press, 1999), p. 562.

[56]The Search Institute has developed a list of forty assets (including community, church and school) that contribute to the healthy development of adolescents. They continually update their materials and research, available at <www.search-institute .org>.

[57]Christian Smith and Melinda Lundquist Denton, *Soul Searching: The Religious and Spiritual Lives of American Teenagers* (New York: Oxford University Press, 2005), p. 115.

[58]Jeffrey Jensen Arnett and Lene Arnett Jensen, "A Congregation of One: Individualized Religious Beliefs Among Emerging Adults," *Journal of Adolescent Research* 17, no. 5 (September 2002): 452.

ever, that adolescents generally follow the beliefs of their parents.[59]

TRANSFORMATION OF THE WHOLE PERSON

The process of the individual to become developmentally "one's own person" requires the transformation of God in his or her life. Jung's understanding of individuation becomes even more compelling at this point. He was not concerned about a focus on the ego as was the fashion of his time; rather, he sought the transformation of the whole person, including the ego. Asked on the BBC interview series *Face to Face* whether he believed in God, he replied, "I do not believe in God. I know."[60]

The work of God in this world is reconciliation—transforming a relationship from one which is broken to one which is reconciled. Meanwhile, the task of adolescence is individuation. Kohut established that this is neither linear nor solely about the work of acquiring a solid sense of self; the work in human development is deeper and seeks *an identity*. Whether acknowledged or not, there is a spiritual component.

James E. Loder contends that Jung had at the center of his thought "religious solutions to the struggles and potential deformities of human development."[61] Loder's own thoughts expand this concept of a religious solution to all understanding of human development.

> Everything in the psychological approach may be seen as the work of the human spirit in its effort to understand and interpret itself. But for all of the analytical power of such theories, their preoccupation with adaptation (important as that may be) prevents them from self-criticism in relation to the more profound issues of human existence. That is, even after we have carefully examined human development from the various standpoints, including criticisms and revisions of the theories, we will not have explicitly said anything of the theological significance. We always must

---

[59]Smith and Denton, *Soul Searching*, p. 170.
[60]James Loder, *The Logic of the Spirit: Human Development in Theological Perspective* (San Francisco: Jossey-Bass, 1998), p. 295.
[61]Ibid., p. 26.

ask, "What is theological about human development?" and allow theology to call the tune if the scope of the inquiry is to be sufficient. Theological consideration must be explicitly brought to bear on these understandings of human development if these understandings are to yield up their theological potential, and if theology is to articulate from within the matrix of human development the meaning and purpose of a lifetime.[62]

By no means does Loder abandon the patriarchs and matriarchs of developmental theories. Rather, he joins them, seeks to understand them and to add an element of completion where they may offer only a partial view. Similar to Erikson, Loder looks at developmental crises throughout the life cycle. Unlike Erikson, however, Loder looks more to the transitional periods—the time between what most developmentalists have called stages, rather than a focus on the stages themselves.[63] Each transition is characterized by an experience of an existential positive and negative. Indeed, it is in this that we find hope in this life and

---

[62]Ibid., p. 27.

[63]James E. Loder, *The Transforming Moment,* 2nd ed. (Colorado Springs: Helmers & Howard, 1989), pp. 126-27. It is important to note that there are criticisms of Loder's approach. James Fowler, while not in complete disagreement, writes, "In Loder's worthy effort to focus on the overall *process* of development, rather than on overly reified stages, I think he falls into a misleading overstatement. . . . If we live more in transitions than in stages, why speak of stages at all?" James Loder and James Fowler, "Conversations of Fowler's *Stages of Faith* and Loder's *The Transforming Moment,*" *Religious Education* 77, no 2 (March-April 1982): 146. Loder answers this very question throughout his writing, particularly here: "It is generally assumed that the transformational process is in the service of and dependent on the stages of development. This is surely true where ego development and inherited structural potentials are concerned, but it is not fundamentally true. The transformational process is more fundamental in that it may (1) transcend the stages, reversing arrested development and reinstating repressed structures; also (2) it may leap ahead by passing stages and establish an imaginative basis for development that incorporates but is not restricted to the so-called normal sequence. In effect, I am suggesting a figure-ground reversal with respect to stages and process. Whereas most studies of development are concerned to map the stages and leave process to itself, this discussion is concerned primarily with the integrity of the process. I want to let the stages emerge in the context of a primary concern for process, first, because we actually spend more of our lives in transition than we do in equilibrium, and second, because stages, as we will see, must finally become a self-liquidating notion if the transformation of human life is to be consummated in Christ" (Loder, *Transforming Moment,* p. 131).

the eschaton as we are being renewed, transformed into the image of God. It is not a stage to be achieved once and for all. It is a lifetime of continual transformation, of continually being renewed. It does not consider salvation a position to be exploited; rather, it takes a position of humility and hope, understanding that not in this fallen, sinful world will transformation be complete but the transformation within individuals and the communal indeed have eternal consequences. Romans 12:2 says, "And do not be conformed to this world, but be transformed by the renewing of your mind, so that you may prove what the will of God is, that which is good and acceptable and perfect" (NASB). It is not in this world that we belong. We are reminded in 2 Corinthians 3:18 that "we all, with unveiled face, beholding as in a mirror the glory of the Lord, are being transformed into the same image from glory to glory, just as from the Lord, the Spirit" (NASB). When our faces are unveiled, when we recognize the void, it is in these moments that we are open to transformation—lest we be lost in the chasm of death.

It is only in the power of Jesus that this transformation is possible, drawing us closer to himself. Recognizing the mandate for not conforming to this world, to continually being transformed, we prevent the danger of thinking we have arrived at a final stage of spiritual development.

Developmental theorists have done a good job at observing and explaining what an individual is experiencing and gaining within each developmental stage. What they have not (or at least not often) mentioned is what is being lost—or more properly, what is being missed. An infant is thrust into this world during birth, gaining independence from the physical attachment to another but losing the security of the womb. A six-month-old finds safety in that which is familiar and experiences the negation at the absence of touch or being able to physically touch that which is familiar. A toddler, reliving these moments of negation, will negate first by shouting every two-year-old's favorite word, "NO!" This toddler is trying to keep the inside inside, and the outside out there, thus the beginnings of Mahler's first individuation. But in the separation is a deep sense of loneliness and the identification of the existential problem. The school-age child is busy with developing intelligence, concrete thinking, seeking community and object relations. The negation comes in being offered only human responses to existential questions.

Loder springs much of his thinking from Chalcedon. "We do not understand that theological answers are brought in to meet human needs, but it is rather the reverse: human needs get their definition and take the form that they do because they already exhibit a longing for a lost reality that is tacitly presupposed by the anguished struggles of the human spirit to find its original ground."[64] The child is already missing what was in the original human relationship.

Adolescence is a renegotiation of space. Loder compares it to an infant who, growing too large for the womb, must move into the world. So too the adolescent grows too large for the confines of the structured life under their primary caregivers. Loder offers four themes which become a part of the core struggle for the adolescent: "1) the inevitability of order, 2) the eventual emergence of disorder, 3) the possibility of new order and 4) the relationality that underlies all forms of order and their explanations."[65] As the adolescent is experiencing these issues—endless choices and no boundaries, making connection and reversal of the negation difficult, which leads to disappointment and what Erikson would call role confusion—Loder offers a theological solution: a potentially infinite horizon that has theological substance, allowing for freedom but resolving the loneliness and negation repeated throughout the stages in life.

As the ego is strengthened, fear emerges that there is nothing—that there is abandonment below the ego. If this is ignored, one may pass through adolescence not with an identity, nor with role confusion, but with a solid self always looking for the meaning underneath. "Recentering the personality beyond the ego in accordance with the exocentric drive (that is, out of egocentrism) of the human spirit, yet without doing away with ego functions" is the transformative task in life which begins in earnest during adolescence.[66]

---

[64]Loder, *Logic of the Spirit*, p. 195.
[65]Ibid., p. 203.
[66]Ibid., p. 232.

TYPES OF NEGATION

Loder further looks to four general types of negation to further understand transformation. The first, calculative negation, "articulates and preserves objectivity and refers primarily to the negation of subjective or egocentric distortions of presumably objective or universal truths."[67] The second, "functional negation," is "negation in and of psychological functions, including both intrapsychic and interpersonal relationships." Existential negation refers to "the negation of one's being. An experience of nothingness as that which forcibly confronts one with one's own nonexistence is as close as one can come to existential negation." Finally, transformational negation refers to "the negation of negation such that a new integration emerges, establishing again over the original negated state of condition."[68] It is the existential and transformational negations with which we are most concerned, though there are certainly implications from the calculative and functional. Loder goes on to say,

> The Christ event—the historical sequence as appropriated by a believer— . . . may be taken as a paradigm of transformation at the level of existential negation. In that appropriation, Christ becomes the adequate mediator for contemporary existential transformation because in his crucifixion he takes ultimate annihilation into himself, and in his resurrection that ultimate negation is negated. In Christ, death dies; by his becoming sin, all sin is canceled. Christ thus creates an ontological gain for those who are in his nature. The crucifixion is a sine qua non of the new being in Christ, lest transformation be truncated in a fantastic aberration from or elevation of one's human existence. Likewise, resurrection is a sine qua non as the opposite of crucifixion, lest God become preeminently an executioner.[69]

---

[67]Loder, *Transforming Moment*, p. 158. Note the compatibility of calculative negation with the concepts of nonfoundationalism. For further exploration, see Stanley Grenz and John R. Franke, eds., *Beyond Foundationalism: Shaping Theology in a Postmodern Context* (Louisville, Ky.: Westminster John Knox, 2001).

[68]Ibid., p. 159.

[69]Ibid., p. 161.

Passionate emergence of existential negation occurs during adolescence. Kenda Creasy Dean has done a tremendous work in this area, exploring passion and its existence in and impact on adolescent life and beyond. She reminds us that "while religious socialization can create Christian-ish youth, by itself it cannot create Christian ones. Christian nurture offers a sense of group affiliation, but—as decades of confirmation graduates bountifully illustrate—this is not the same thing as a passionate commitment of faith."[70] The negation of the negation occurs as an adolescent experiences a relationship "more powerful than the void. . . . In this experience of what David Ford calls the 'overflowing soteriology of abundance,' teenage 'nobodies' become confident 'somebodies,' 'created in Christ from before the beginning of the world' with an identity that cannot be taken from them."[71] There is a silver lining to what seems so difficult.

TRANSFORMATION, NEGATION AND COMMUNITY

In keeping with Kohut's interdependence, transformation is never about the individual alone. Herbert Anderson reminds us that

> most societies of the world begin their consideration of the person with the community. . . . [James] Lapsley is correct when he insists that there is, in fact, no individual gospel—"only a salvation by participation in which the identity of the individual is lost." There is, for Lapsley, an inescapable communal dimension to being human that corrects the individualistic anthropology of pastoral theology.[72]

---

[70]Kenda Creasy Dean, *Practicing Passion: Youth and the Quest for a Passionate Church* (Grand Rapids: Eerdmans, 2004), p. 147.

[71]Dana Wright with Kenda Creasy Dean, "Youth, Passion, and Intimacy in the Context of Koinonia," in *Redemptive Transformation in Practical Theology: Essays in Honor of James Loder,* ed. Dana Wright and John Kuentzel (Grand Rapids: Eerdmans, 2004), p. 164; quoting David Ford, *Self and Salvation: Being Transformed* (Cambridge: Cambridge University Press, 1999), pp. 113-14.

[72]Herbert Anderson, "The Recovery of Soul," in *The Treasure of Earthen Vessels: Explorations in Theological Anthropology,* ed. Brian Childs and David W. Waanders (Louisville, Ky.: Westminster John Knox, 1994), pp. 216-17. James Lapsley spent a career exploring theological understandings of human life and experience. For a further look at his understanding of salvation see James Lapsley, *Salvation and Health: The*

This is good news for youth groups! Transformation is not an isolated experience but rather one that takes place in and requires interdependence in community. There is a reciprocal relationship which occurs: as individuals are transformed, so too is the community. As the community is transformed, so too are individuals. The second of the three strands of existence, the communal, is interdependent with both the individual and the eternal. "Transformation occurs when the social group, as the Body of Christ, can come to say, 'we, not we, but the *koinonia* of Christ.' Once again a dialectical identity is given, in which both the unity of the group and the particularity of its members are deepened simultaneously."[73]

Individuation—becoming one's own person—is the developmental task of the adolescent stage within a lifelong process of differentiation. This is not an isolated journey of growth toward rugged individualism; adolescents grow within their environment, its influences, structures, pathology and salubrity. With guidance and nurturance, adolescents mature. Ideally, as an adolescent moves from childhood to adulthood, authentic connections are made both with their community and with the eternal. Youth ministers have the privilege of walking with adolescents on this journey.

In order to best accompany adolescents on this journey, the youth minister needs more than an understanding of psychological and biological developmental issues. An understanding of the culture is both crucial and elusive. In the following chapter, the key role of culture will be explored.

QUESTIONS FOR FURTHER THOUGHT

1. How have you seen lengthening adolescence or emerging adulthood influencing youth ministry?

2. In what ways might youth workers help an adolescent with their task of individuation?

Interlocking Processes of Life (Philadelphia: Westminster Press, 1972).

[73]Russell Haitch, "Trampling Down Death by Death," in *Redemptive Transfomation in Practical Theology: Essays in Honor of James Loder,* ed. Dana Wright and John Kuentzel (Grand Rapids: Eerdmans, 2004), p. 48.

3. What makes an adolescent developmentally ready to hear about God, to come to belief that God exists and to build a relationship with God for life?

4. Adolescent development is a part of the psychosocial portion of the bilingual conversation. In which steps of the pastoral cycle do you see this as needing to be present? How?

5. How do you see development and transformation relating to one another and in parallel to one another?

4

A CLARIFICATION OF CONTEXT

UNDERSTANDING YOUTH CULTURE

The automobile is replacing the kitchen as the gathering place for the family unit.
Conversation takes place in the car as it connects the dots of the family's social
system, not at the kitchen table.

DIANA GARLAND, *FAMILY MINISTRY*

If I gave you my life, you would drop it. Wouldn't you?

THE ENGLISH PATIENT

Piglet sidled up to Pooh from behind. "Pooh!" he whispered. "Yes, Piglet?" "Nothing,"
said Piglet, taking Pooh's paw. "I just wanted to be sure of you."

THE HOUSE AT POOH CORNER

THE ENTIRE ROOM WAS STUNNED. One teenager called out, "We need to pray for the Jacksons!" All of the students nodded in agreement; meanwhile, the adults looked sheepishly at one another, wondering if this was real or not.

It was the day Michael Jackson died. I was at camp with a group of amazing teenagers. There was no judgment, no mocking; the request was sincere. There was a uniform connection with something much bigger than themselves, and it centered on a musician they had never met. Michael Jackson was central to popular culture, and popular culture is the playground of adolescents. Jackson's death was a rare glimpse into their world in a raw and unifying moment.

I love spending time with my students. Of course, spending time takes on a variety of forms: basketball games, volleyball games, choir concerts and band competitions are among the usual suspects. I look at art portfolios, short films and spoken word, both things they have created and things they enjoy. We hang out. I also get to share some of what I love. Any student I've had for any length of time knows I love U2, the blues, hiking, cooking and (not often enough) surfing. We share our interests.

I don't pretend to know every new song or dress in the latest fashion trend—I don't want to be that creepy adult who tries too hard to fit in. I do, however, want to be able to speak to my students and learn from them. They have a great deal to share. We go to movies as a group and then talk about how it made us feel or what messages were being conveyed. We shop together and discuss both fashion and who made the clothes. We eat together and talk about ethnicity and family traditions. We listen to music and talk about likes, dislikes and the struggle when you like a song with some words that clearly do not honor God—even if the overall message does.

Culture is a blend of stable and ever-changing elements. We can never know it all, but we can know some. When it comes to culture, often we do not even recognize our own until we have a close encounter with a culture that is different. The result is a clash of cultures and heightened awareness of the other. Ideally, healthy reflection also takes place, and one's own culture is brought into sharper relief. As youth workers, some of the most powerful tools we have are listening, watching, and experiencing a real and vital adolescent culture. We can build authentic relationships as we learn the questions they have. These very questions form the foundation of our helping them to line up Christian beliefs with the way they live.

This is not unique to the Christian community. Culture in general comprises rules, norms and values. Jeffrey Jensen Arnett says that "cultural beliefs include both the beliefs that constitute a culture's symbolic inheritance and the norms and moral standards that arise from those beliefs."[1] As youth workers, we consider the culture of adolescence. Pamela Erwin sets this in context, stating, "Because of the changes that occur during puberty, young people are ripe for learning the rules, norms and standards being communicated through their interactions with family, friends and communities."[2] Culture is all around us as adults and adolescents. It is the water in which we swim, the air we breathe.

Adolescents do not grow up in a vacuum. In fact, one of the markers of adolescence is the entrance and transition into a world of adolescents, known as *youth culture*. Youth culture is the second half of the psychosocial language required for a bilingual approach in forming a practical theology particular to adolescence. The relationship between culture and adolescents is one of socialization. Adolescents are socialized and socialize the culture around them. Erwin writes:

> Adolescent development, then, is the process of evolving conception that takes place during the teenage years. This definition denotes the reciprocal relationship between a young person and her environment, meaning there is a back-and-forth, give-and-take dynamic to the interactions she has with her environment. On one hand, the personal experiences and feedback she receives in that environment, including growth in cognitive and emotional capabilities, shape how the young person perceives of her world. On the other hand the young person shapes the environment through her interactions, giving feedback and response in a variety of ways that meaningfully shape her surroundings.[3]

Youth culture is not only an influencing factor on young people, it is created and re-created with each generation. While the details

---

[1]Jeffrey Jensen Arnett, *Adolescent and Emerging Adulthood: A Cultural Approach*, 4th ed. (Upper Saddle River, N.J.: Prentice Hall, 2010), p. 93.
[2]Pamela Erwin, *A Critical Approach to Youth Culture: Its Influence and Implications for Ministry* (Grand Rapids: Zondervan, 2010), p. 118.
[3]Ibid., p. 108.

change and nuances occur, there are consistent categories within cultural studies.

Fluency in the consistent categories within adolescent culture is valuable to the exploration phase of the pastoral cycle. Individuation, the primary task of adolescent self-formation, not only does not presume isolation; it rules isolation out as a healthy environment for growth. Culture (including popular culture) is no longer a byproduct with little influence on the daily lives of those in society. Postmodernity has brought this conversation to the forefront of much discussion revolving around youth.[4]

The origins of trends in youth culture can be elusive. Cultural trends move from novelty to normative. Youth culture is formed by and shapes the adolescents of the time.[5] The labyrinth of culture is dense with moving walls. There are no rigid boundaries within culture set for all time—yet there are common understandings, building blocks which can be identified. How the blocks are assembled, colored, lit and displayed alters slightly with each individual constituting the whole. Loren Wilkinson says culture can be seen "in the broadest

---

[4]For further reading on postmodernism see Stanley Grenz, *A Primer on Postmodernism* (Grand Rapids: Eerdmans, 1996). While not used often in conversation with an adolescent, terms such as *youth, teenagers* and *adolescents* are commonly used across anthropological, sociological and psychological writings. *Millennials* will be used to refer to the group of adolescents at the time of this writing. See Neil Howe and William Strauss, *Millennials Rising: The Next Generation* (New York: Vintage Books, 2000).

[5]The seemingly numerous reasons for the shift in culture are as of yet absent from the majority of research. The results, however, provide rich ground for discovery and interpretation. "Contemporary youth have increasingly become more alienated from mainstream social institutions that have traditionally provided them with value references and normative support. As a consequence, growing proportions of young people have put little, if any, investment in these institutions. In the United States, a large portion of young people come from inner city, low-income minority families that exist within a community context of disempowerment, limited access to resources, and daily violence, crime and substance abuse. Such youth often respond to their marginalization in ways that further distance them from prosocial sources of support. In the context of a culture that has become increasingly more complex, diverse, and pluralistic, confronting challenges and making the life choices that define an individual's sense of personal (i.e., Who am I?) and moral identity (i.e., What do I believe in?) has become a formidable task, even for the most resilient of young people" (Laura Ferrer-Wreder et al., "Promoting Identity Development in Marginalized Youth," *Journal of Adolescent Research* 17, no. 2 [March 2002]: 168-69).

sense (as) everything that people do with creation."[6] He goes on to make the distinction between high culture ("the most honored works and ways of a civilization, the sorts of things we enshrine today in concert halls and art galleries, or promote through liberal arts education"), folk culture ("all of the unique patterns of behavior of a particular people or society . . . [referring] not to the works of specialized producers of high culture (musicians, poets, painters, actors) but to the unique flavor of a particular people's way of life" and popular culture ("something midway between high and folk though overlapping with both").[7] Consequently, before stepping ahead, a closer look at culture in general is needed.[8]

GOD OF CULTURE

James Wm. McClendon Jr. offers useful insight into the quest for an understanding of culture. He follows an accepted definition of anthropology: culture is a "set of meaningful practices, dominant attitudes, and characteristic ways of doing things that typify a community (or a society or a civilization)."[9] With James Smith, McClendon offers an alternative to the imperialist ("one culture") and the pluralist ("many cultures"); their "perspectivism"

> regards convictional conflict as expected, but not inevitable, fundamental but not ultimate, enduring but not inherently ineradicable.[10]

McClendon defines *convictions* as "the enduring, basic beliefs that typify cultures."[11] Convictions as a concept prevent a number of difficulties otherwise present.

---

[6]Loren Wilkinson, "Culture," in *The Complete Book of Everyday Christianity*, ed. Robert Banks and R. Paul Stevens (Downers Grove, Ill.: InterVarsity Press, 1997), p. 257.

[7]Ibid.

[8]See appendix B for a brief discussion of the range of perspectives on culture.

[9]James Wm. McClendon Jr., *Systematic Theology*, vol. 3, *Witness* (Nashville: Abingdon, 2000), p. 50.

[10]James Wm. McClendon Jr. and James M. Smith, *Convictions: Defusing Religious Relativism* (Valley Forge, Penn.: Trinity Press International, 1994), p. 9.

[11]McClendon, *Witness*, p. 54.

Working with such a notion as "convictions" (or one of its cousins
such as "presuppositions," "incorrigible assumptions," "metaphysi-
cal beliefs"—no single term for this widely recognized phenomenon is in common use), it is possible to pry cultural relativity in its
healthiest sense (our "perspectivism") away from cultural imperi-
alism (the view that one's own culture has it all right all the time,
culturally speaking, so that other cultures had better fall in line)
and also pry it away from despairing cultural *apartheid* (the view
that one's culture really has nothing to do with some other or others, and vice versa, so that everyone's best hope is to stay segre-
gated). Perspectivism makes room for rival truth-claims and other
rival value-claims. It also recognizes the ways in which variant
cultures encounter one another, clash, combine, persuade, and are
persuaded, with the possibility that new cultural forms may in-
herit and appropriate the old ones.[12]

As a Christian, McClendon concludes with an understanding of
convictions that leads to theology and ultimately God. Culture is the
realm in which God works to reconcile the world to himself.

God, by His servant redeems the world from its self-deceit, il-
lusions, [and] lies. Thus part of the task is to recognize the cultural sin which mars (though it can never efface) divine creation. The footprints of God along the shore lead to an execution
site. It is a cross. Theology of culture finds that cross and its
neighboring grave—but it finds them empty. He is risen. The
resurrection is a signal of hope calling culture on to its full
redemption.[13]

A shift of the emphasis is needed. McClendon is focused on the "sin
which mars . . . divine creation"; another valid perspective is that of
looking for the divine creation within a marred world. One of McClendon's strengths is his belief that "God is the God of culture as well as of
nature; therefore culture's hope like nature's destiny lies in the gospel of

---

[12]Ibid.
[13]Ibid., p. 55.

God's grace."[14] As God is the God *of* culture, he is already present *in* culture. While his presence may not always be easily recognizable, culture is neither worthless nor beyond redemption; on the contrary, culture is often the revelatory point of redemption for both the individual and communal.

Likewise, there is no culture-free approach to life and all that it entails. This includes the reading of Scripture. Culture's proclivity toward revelation is complemented by specific hermeneutical reads of culture. A sort of reciprocal socialization takes place, such that any exegesis of a cultural phenomenon can never be truly objective. "Just as there is no culture-free reading of the biblical text and no culture-free construction of Christian theology, so also there can be no 'theology-free' reading of culture and cultural artifacts."[15] Each Christian cannot help but filter culture through a particular tradition. Most often this is the tradition in which he or she was raised or discipled. Youth culture is no exception.

COMMON CULTURE: YOUTH AND DEVELOPMENT

Youth culture is full of its own particular set of convictions. In contrast to high art—"the institutions and practices, genres and terms [of which]," Paul Willis contends, "are currently categories of exclusion more than of inclusion"[16]—youth culture creates its own canon, open to as many "arts" as possible. While the young are not often involved in "high culture," they are involved in a symbolic creativity which larger society often overlooks or disregards. Common culture is that approach which considers the everyday activities as vibrant and expressive of actual and potential cultural significance. Willis goes on to suggest that while "most young people's lives are not involved with the arts" per se, they are nevertheless "actually full of expressions, signs and symbols through which individuals and groups seek creatively to establish their

---

[14]Ibid., p. 56.
[15]Stanley Grenz and John R. Franke, eds., *Beyond Foundationalism: Shaping Theology in a Postmodern Context* (Louisville, Ky.: Westminster John Knox, 2001), p. 159.
[16]Paul Willis, *Common Culture* (Boulder, Colo.: Westview Press, 1993), p. 1.

presence, identity and meaning."[17] Youth have life spaces and social choices which constitute their culture, including

> personal styles and choices of clothes; selective and active use of music, TV, magazines; decoration of bedrooms; the rituals of romance and subcultural styles; the style, banter and drama of friendship groups; music-making and dance.[18]

Where it was once only discussed within an exclusive and limited sector of society, culture is now recognized as being present in some form or fashion in every corner of the world, existing for specific segments of the world delineated by such boundaries as interest or age. Youth culture is just such an entity.[19]

What Loder did at length in connecting spirituality with adolescent development, Willis does (seemingly unknowingly) in succinct terms connecting culture and adolescent development. Symbolic creativity is present everyday in the necessities of life creating and reflecting culture. Willis wrestles with what culture is through the question "What exactly is produced by this symbolic creativity?" He offers a triumvirate response.

> Firstly and perhaps most important, they produce and reproduce individual identities—who and what "I am" and could become. . . . Secondly symbolic work and creativity place identities in larger wholes. Identities do not stand alone above history, beyond history. They are related in time, place and things. . . . Memberships of race, class, gender, age and region are not only learned, they're lived and experimented with. . . . Third and finally, symbolic work and especially creativity develop and affirm our active senses of our own vital capacities, the powers of the self and how they might be applied to the cultural world.[20]

---

[17]Ibid.

[18]Ibid., p. 2.

[19]For a longitudinal look at youth culture from a British and American perspective, read Jon Savage, *TeenAge: The Creation of Youth Culture* (New York: Viking Press, 2007).

[20]Willis, *Common Culture*, pp. 11-12.

Willis offers a way for the individual to develop culturally within a greater context, recognizing not only the potentiality but also the reality of a connection with something much greater than their own space and time.[21] There is a sense of the eternal as one looks at what occurs as a result of symbolic creativity.

Symbolic creativity exists in real life in particular contexts, not merely as abstraction. As a symbolic activity, it carries with it the obligation of transformation, or what Willis calls "grounded aesthetics":

> Grounded aesthetics are the specifically creative and dynamic moments of a whole process of cultural life, of cultural birth and rebirth. To know the cultural world, our relationship to it, and ultimately to know ourselves, it is necessary not merely to be in it but to change—however minutely—that cultural world. This is a making specific—in relation to the social group or individual and its conditions of life—of the ways in which the received natural and social world is made human to them and made, to however small a degree (even if finally symbolic), controllable by them.[22]

This, in very different language, is the pastoral cycle. An experience (no matter how slight) is followed by exploration and then reflection leading to action (no matter how slight).[23] Symbolic activity is (potentially) a secularized version of practical theology. Willis uses ethnography to transcend mere theoretical offerings. His grounded aesthetic is, in particular, a focus on whom he continually calls "the young." It is the youth seeking identity both individually and corporately who offer culture within everyday life occurrences.

---

[21]This concept of identity forming in context is affirmed in research. "The tendency to evaluate the self as significant to others may have two functions. First, perceived mattering has the potential to affectively and cognitively inform individuals of their sense of belonging to others, which operates to reduce marginality or the feeling of being peripheral to the social context. The function of relatedness may work in coordination with a second function, a sense of meaning for existence" (Sheila Marshall, "Do I Matter? Construct Validation of Adolescents' Perceived Mattering to Parents and Friends," *Journal of Adolescence* 24 [2001]: 474).

[22]Willis, *Common Culture*, pp. 21-22.

[23]Paul Ballard and John Pritchard, *Practical Theology in Action: Christian Thinking in the Service of Church and Society* (London: SPCK, 1996), pp. 77-78.

MILLENNIALS

There is no way to write the definitive work on adolescents, as they are just that: adolescents—ever growing and changing. They will have loved something one year and consider it old school by next. They are typically more on top of technology, movies, music and fashion than any other demographic.

While change is inevitable and each new generation is dynamic, there are principles which transcend. For the following section, I will focus on those born between 1985 and the early 2000s.[24] A great deal has been discussed with regard to youth culture in recent years. Within many Christian youth ministry circles, Walt Mueller is considered to be an expert in current youth culture.[25] As is common, Mueller never offers a definition of culture; rather, he assumes the definition is embedded in the very fabric of those whom he is addressing. His offering is best understood by looking at categories: music, media, friends, love and sex, materialism, alcohol and drugs, and emotions. On a much larger scale, Neil Howe and William Strauss have set the tone for what many think about Millennials.[26] To their credit, they don't claim to be identifying characteristics for all within this age group, and they admit to a very limited sampling. They devote an entire book, however, to analyzing data and offering their interpretation and comparison to past generations. Their influence knows almost no bounds; in *Group Magazine*, a popular magazine across mainline denominations to aid and inform youth ministers, Kelli Trujillo relied on Howe and Strauss's contentions to develop three

---

[24] The principles and categories found here will be relevant long after the specifics. As of this writing, the eldest of the generation to come are currently on the cusp of early adolescence. Consequently, there is no research yet. Largely based around economic trends, I imagine the next generation to include less of a sense of entitlement and be open to concepts of hope and provision in ways not recently seen.

[25] Through his organization the Center for Parent and Youth Understanding, Walt Mueller offers a variety of services and information in a timely manner. In particular is the weekly update sent via e-mail and the constantly updated web page found at <www.cpyu.org>. See also Walt Mueller, *Youth Culture 101* (Grand Rapids: Zondervan, 2007).

[26] Neil Howe and William Strauss, *The Fourth Turning: An American Prophecy* (New York: Broadway Books, 1998).

strategies for meeting these "optimistic, multi-tasking, world-saving" adolescents.[27] According to Trujillo, these kids want to give back and do it wisely so as to not waste any more of their already taxed time. They believe they can change the world and are going to do it whether we as adults choose to help or not. The secular world tends to accept this optimistic view, which belies a constant stream of information that tells of a world in chaos.[28]

What is lurking below the surface of contemporary adolescence is

---

[27]Kelli Trujillo, "Strategies for Reaching Today's Kids: Three Rules About Millennials," *Group Magazine,* January 2, 2002, pp. 49-52. Interestingly, Trujillo identifies Howe and Strauss as "two respected sociologists" (p. 49), but in their own book they make no such claim: Neil Howe identifies himself as a senior advisor to the Concord Coalition and senior policy advisor to the Blackstone Group; his degrees are in history and economics; William Strauss identifies himself as the cofounder and director of Capital Steps (a political cabaret), a former policy director for Congress, and author of two musicals on teen themes. Even more interesting is the openness with which Howe and Strauss reveal their research methodology. They offer in the notes a list of newspaper articles, websites and other materials they drew from to compile their research. Their own survey work consisted of surveying two hundred elementary, middle and high school teachers in twelve schools in Fairfax County, Virginia, and a survey of 660 students (graduating class of June 2000) in four public high schools in the same Fairfax County. Given the limited scope of this research, it's remarkable how much their viewpoint has influenced adult-driven approaches to adolescents—and not limited to ministry. Chap Clark notes that "the empirical research on the state of contemporary adolescence is so reliant on self-report questionnaires, government-funded and administered studies, generic school surveys, and other mass attempts to understand the trends and attitudes of teenagers that the underlying reality of their daily lives seems to be missing from the reams of data that fuel the academics" (Chap Clark, "Entering Their World: A Qualitative Look at the Changing Face of Contemporary Adolescence," *The Journal of Youth Ministry* 1, no. 1 [Fall 2002]: 10).

[28]The cover story for the June 3, 2002, issue of *Newsweek* defined the Millennial "Gamma Girls" as confident and self-assured rather than cynical and demotivated. See Susannah Meadows, "Meet the GAMMA Girls," *Newsweek,* June 3, 2002, pp. 44-51. This same positive optimistic trend is offered in *The Ambitious Generation,* in which the authors study 7,000 teenagers; overwhelmingly the Millennial generation views a world with unlimited opportunities and possibilities allowing them to be hopeful, optimistic and ambitious; though lacking in direction, they are seen as ambitious compared to adolescents of the 1950s. The cultural shift within gender issues alone, however, is enough to skew this interpretation. While the raw data of the research is not bad, the interpretation is rendered moot. See Barbara Schneider and David Stevenson, *The Ambitious Generation: America's Teenagers Motivated but Directionless* (New Haven, Conn.: Yale University Press, 1999).

vastly different from what is being reported in surveys. Three exceptions have made an impact at varying levels in the last decade.[29]

Elinor Burkett moved from New York to Minnesota to spend the school year at Prior Lake High School. Her goal was to hear from students what is really going on, not simply what they are willing to report on a survey. What remains consistent with the stories offered from various students is not the overwhelming optimism and hopefulness adults have come to be delighted by in surface reporting, but the adolescent world itself is "another planet" few are invited to see.[30]

With even greater depth (aided by six years of research, three of which were with eight students in particular), Patricia Hersch presents *A Tribe Apart*. This is the insight not of someone who carried on a superficial conversation or looked only through piles of research. In her preface alone, she succinctly refutes what is being offered by more popularized but cursory reports on current youth culture. She invites us to "look more closely. Beneath these remarkable displays of togetherness, it is clear that adolescents today inhabit a world largely unknown to adults. . . . Picture-perfect suburbs and small towns mask an insidious reality: Today's teens are a tribe apart."[31]

In the *Frontline* special titled "Growing Up Online,"[32] research from both Harvard and Berkeley are used to corroborate works identifying the pessimistic and often secret lives and attitudes of teens. Those are all valid pieces of the puzzle, but they do not, they cannot, show the entire picture.

---

[29]Several book have been written in this vein. While the two in the main text are the most prominent, the following offer valuable insight and perspective as well: Adrian Nicole LeBlanc, *Random Family: Love, Drugs, Trouble and Coming of Age in the Bronx* (New York, Scribner, 2003); Joanna Lipper, *Growing Up Fast* (New York: Picador, 2003); Neil Postman, *The Disappearance of Childhood* (New York: Vintage Books, 1994).

[30]Elinor Burkett, *Another Planet: A Year in the Life of a Suburban High School* (New York: HarperCollins, 2001).

[31]Patricia Hersch, *A Tribe Apart: A Journey into the Heart of American Adolescence* (New York: Ballantine, 1999), p. viii. The strength of this book is its in-depth walk with adolescents. Its weakness is in being a very narrow scope with limited application. Still, this qualitative work offers more depth than surveys.

[32]"Growing Up Online," *Frontline*, 90 minutes, aired January 22, 2008.

MINISTERIAL PERSPECTIVE

Journalists and social scientists are not the only ones taking notice of the disparity between the surface and deeper levels of adolescent life. Malan Nel, a veteran youth worker in South Africa and a professor at Pretoria University, offers an outsider's look at adolescents in the United States.

> On top of what they have always had to struggle with, youth now also are in desperate need for understanding by the people who helped create the society youth now call "my world." They still have to find identity, they still suffer neglect, broken relationships, abuse, [and] they are still exposed to drugs, money, power, racism. The "heavy extra" is that they have to do all of this, find themselves, where nothing is clear cut.[33]

Nel offers a sobering reminder that the changes which have occurred did not replace former struggles; rather, they added to them while removing supports no longer fully present. Kenda Creasy Dean similarly asserts that "postmodern young people reside in a milieu of contradictions that do not reduce to neat explanations."[34]

Answers are no longer clearly defined. Individuals and institutions have largely given up their role as guide; adolescents have been left to figure it out for themselves, while many adults wonder what has changed with the adolescents of today. What has changed is that on many levels adolescents have been abandoned.[35] The difficulty comes in trying to tease this concept out while more money, media attention, marketing and focus is being directed toward the young in society than ever before.[36] It is, however, difficult to quench one's thirst at a fire hydrant.

---

[33]Malan Nel, "Serving Them Back: Youth Evangelism in a Secular and Postmodern World," *Journal of Youth and Theology* 1, no. 1 (April 2002): 69-70.

[34]Kenda Creasy Dean, "X-Files and Unknown Gods: The Search for Truth with Postmodern Adolescents," *American Baptist Quarterly* 19, no. 1 (March 2000): 17.

[35]The language of *abandonment* is borrowed from David Elkind, *The Hurried Child: Growing Up Too Fast Too Soon*, 25th anniv. ed. (Cambridge, Mass.: De Capo Press, 2006).

[36]See, for example, Teenage Research Unlimited at <www.teenresearch.com> and <www.marketresearch.com>.

Creasy Dean acknowledges as much:

> For all the "truths" of their media-saturated lives, they remain frustratingly far removed from the answers they seek. The deluge of facts laid out for public inspection has not shed light on who they are, alleviated their pain, or quelled their desire to belong. Their mission still is to discover the inalienable truth about themselves.[37]

We then find ourselves not only looking at core questions—Who am I? Where do I belong? Do I matter?—we also must recognize adolescents trying to make sense of the worlds in which they live.

THE RELATIONSHIP BETWEEN ADULTS AND ADOLESCENTS

The identification of adolescents as feeling first lost and then the almost palpable feeling of being abandoned drives them into a frenetic push for affirmation, loyalty and solid relationships. This assertion is confirmed in the work of Christian Smith and Melinda Lundquist Denton, who remind us of the profound change from a society where young people were "closely involved in the productive activities of and supervised by the watchful eyes of adults" to one where a structural disconnection is present between adults and teenagers.[38] Diana Garland offers this startling analogy: "Children have become an expensive hobby, something to be enjoyed in spare time if the family can afford it, like golf or another expensive pastime."[39]

Adults changed the rules, watched the reaction of their children turned adolescents and wonder why they do not behave the way they did at that age. Rather than reaching out, as a society, we have blamed the victim with few willing to even listen long enough to recognize that teenagers are smart enough to play the game. What is reported on surveys and observed on the surface is a beautiful façade hiding the world beneath. It is true that resilience is present, but the long-

---

[37]Creasy Dean, "X-Files and Unknown Gods," p. 17.
[38]Christian Smith and Melinda Lundquist Denton, *Soul Searching: The Religious and Spiritual Lives of American Teenagers* (New York: Oxford University Press, 2005), pp. 182-86.
[39]Diana Garland, *Family Ministry: A Comprehensive Guide* (Downers Grove, Ill.: InterVarsity Press, 1999), p. 559.

term effects of this seeming optimism and outward ambition is lengthened adolescence and a further abandonment by an impatient adult world.[40]

There is, however, an upside to this ostensibly bleak picture. Values are changing in small increments. Garland observes,

> Today it is *right* for parents to be involved in their children's lives, even if it occasionally compromises their work performance. This is especially true for fathers, who had for several decades been seen as peripheral to their children's well-being but are being re-discovered as necessary ingredients in the lives of healthy, well-adjusted children.[41]

Parents needing the assurance that their time and attention is wanted can be comforted by recent findings that their kids value them in their lives.[42] There is an openness to spirituality and working through values and beliefs—though not quite the direct route of following in one's family tradition of faith. The combination of ease of availability of information and a climate of understanding and tolerance for any alternative beliefs makes values more negotiable than in the past. This does not mean that they are not important, simply that they may not look like what adults have come to expect.

> Because young people view it as both their right and their responsibility to form their beliefs and values independently of their parents, they pick and choose from the ideas they discover as they go along and combine them to form their own unique, individualized set of beliefs, "an a la carte belief system."[43]

---

[40]Ironically, huge portions of the adult world constitute movements and industries striving for not the young themselves to be celebrated but the nostalgic image of youth and all its accoutrements as idealized by those abandoning the actual young of the day.

[41]Garland, *Family Ministry,* p. 32.

[42]Sheila Marshall, "Do I Matter? Construct Validation of Adolescents' Perceived Mattering to Parents and Friends," *Journal of Adolescence* 24 (2001): 487.

[43]Jeffrey Jensen Arnett and Lene Arnett Jensen, "A Congregation of One: Individualized Religious Beliefs Among Emerging Adults," *Journal of Adolescent Research* 17, no. 5 (September 2002): 464.

In a world where they have been largely abandoned, Millennials are surprisingly hopeful; they do have an interest in family, community and a value system they can believe. They are not as naively optimistic as some portray them to be. Nor are they refusing interaction. In fact, they continue to report relationships both with parents, peers and other adults as supremely important.[44] What they refuse is surface-level, insincere manipulation, as they have watched the adults in their world become self-absorbed and hypocritical. They will turn to one another to forge the path to adulthood if they do not find it in those around them. Their convictions are strong and present in this world.

There are many arenas that offer insight through examples. Music, fashion, TV, Internet, sports, movies and advertising are all points of distinct focus both reflective of and influential on the adolescent world. The young are sophisticated readers of media and image. The Internet in particular has offered the ability to have a blurring of the lines between consumption and production, between reality and fantasy, as entire lives are created and re-created through personal interactive pages. Adolescents value community and look for ways to have a primary experience including interaction. Willis, when identifying symbolic creativity, gives particular attention to the cinema. "The cinema seems to make film viewing a much more social experience. . . . Young people take pleasure out of interacting with one another when watching films. There is a grounded aesthetic in laughing, clapping together."[45] Hang out with any group of teenagers and you quickly recognize another point of connection that creates a marker for community: the practice of quoting movie lines.[46] YouTube moves this into a whole new realm, allowing teens to create a movie, seek a wide audience, solicit instant feedback and adjust the work they have done accordingly. It is a multimedia conversation where individuals seek to know and be known.

---

[44]Smith and Denton again remind us that "the structural disconnect of youth from adults may generate in at least some youth a hunger for meaningful relationships with mature adults, for many youth do in fact desire the boundaries, teaching, direction, wisdom and caring that adults can offer." Smith and Denton, *Soul Searching*, p. 186.

[45]Willis, *Common Culture*, p. 64.

[46]Jack Gabig, *Youth, Religion and Film* (Cambridge: YTC Press, 2007).

Jon Boorstin offers three major perspectives for effective cinema: the voyeur's eye, the vicarious eye and the visceral eye. "The voyeur's eye is the mind's eye, not the heart's, the dispassionate observer, watching out of a kind of generic human curiosity. It is not only skeptical, it is easily bored."[47] The voyeuristic approach offers a solid, logical story. It is the element that requires an element of believability (not necessarily reality; a well-done fantasy film allows for suspension of reality). It looks for surprise and twists but rejects incongruent assumptions that do not respect the intelligence of the audience. Emotions are drawn in by the vicarious eye, which

> mixes our yearnings to matter—to be taken seriously, to have our emotions count—with our need to please others, to read the slightest shift in their feelings and accommodate to it. The vicarious eye puts our heart in the actor's body: we feel what the actor feels, but we judge it for ourselves.[48]

The *vicarious experience* then moves us from the cognitive to the emotive,[49] and finally to the *visceral experience*. This moves beyond plot or feeling "what the character feels but to feel your own emotions, to have the experience yourself, directly. . . . The character is a conduit for the viewer's feelings, not the other way around."[50] This is where the point-of-view shots (POVs) come into their own. You don't watch a person fall from a cliff, you see the cliff rush past as you experience the fall. It is the gut reaction, what Boorstin defines as sensation over emotion.

Not only can these three perspectival approaches shed light on every area of adolescent life, but they also speak poignantly to ministry. As Craig Detweiler observes, "If the best movies engaged the entire person, then shouldn't the best churches involve our brains, our hearts and

---

[47]Jon Boorstin, *Making Movies Work: Thinking Like a Filmmaker* (Los Angeles: Silman-James Press, 1995), p. 13. Thanks to Craig Detweiler, a filmmaker himself, fellow Fuller student and now graduate and advising friend. He introduced me to Boorstin and offered priceless insight as to the connections with theology.
[48]Ibid., p. 67.
[49]Boorstin goes on to illustrate this, saying, "The vicarious experience is not bound by iron bands of logic but by silken cords of emotional truth." Ibid.
[50]Ibid., p. 110.

our bodies?"[51] Movies which hit at each of the three perspectives within the course of 90-120 minutes engage the whole person, transport, and ultimately transform the individual and collective audiences as they share the experience. There is a sense of the spiritual in this transformative experience.

MILLENNIALS AND MOVIES

While common threads may twist through films in general, there are those which are outside of the actual life of the film as well. The experience of sitting in a theater with others, participation in the hype leading to the release of the film and the word of mouth following the film's release are but a few of these threads. With the advent of social networking, teens announce their own video productions via Facebook, MySpace and Twitter, and then wait to go viral. They check repeatedly for the viewer count and for comments from viewers. In contrast to contentions by people such as Brian Godawa, who sees in postmodernity (which would include Millennials) a general denial of objectivity that deconstructs individuals' identity as they are engulfed and reconstructed by society,[52] Millennials in fact have a healthy sense of individual identity. It is not created in isolation , however, but incubates and is influenced within context and at times in spite of context. The common culture of adolescents provides voyeuristic, vicarious and visceral ways of peering into the multifaceted dimensions of development.

Culture, as it relates, shapes and surrounds adolescents, is ever changing for youth ministers. Its usefulness is as a point of entry to the communal realm, a sort of modern canon that helps to form the questions within practical theology that are pertinent to adolescents in their current context. Culture, along with adolescent development, makes up the psychosocial language for the bilingual discussion, in which the youth minister can represent the counterculture of followers of Christ— not "Christianity versus the world" but a true counterculture that ex-

---

[51]Craig Detweiler, "The Holy Trinity of Filmmaking," paper presented at City of Angels Film Festival, Los Angeles, November 1, 2002.
[52]Brian Godawa, *Hollywood Worldviews: Watching Films with Wisdom and Discernment* (Downers Grove, Ill.: InterVarsity Press, 2002), p. 86.

poses, examines, and comes into dialogue with and understands the values influencing adolescents. Youth ministers facilitate the confrontation of life patterns that are destructive to love, justice, mercy and ultimately reconciliation, instead encouraging transformation in all developmental areas of life toward reconciliation and becoming an authentic follower of Christ.

It is from theology that the human dimensions of the individual, communal and eternal spring. The development of each, in relation to one another, is reflective of creation, the Trinity and the work of God in the world. In the next chapter, the language of the theologian will be considered at length.

QUESTIONS FOR FURTHER THOUGHT

1. What about adolescent culture excites you?

2. What is your reaction at reading "God is the God of culture as well as of nature"?

3. How has your cultural lens affected your understanding of Scripture? Christian doctrines? Following Jesus?

4. In what ways might youth workers help adolescents be wise participants within culture?

5. What are the favorite elements of pop culture among your youth? How do you currently interact with your students around these elements?

6. Adolescent culture is a part of the psychosocial portion of the bilingual conversation. In which steps of the pastoral cycle do you see this as needing to be present? How?

5

THEOLOGICAL INFLUENCES

FAITH WITH UNDERSTANDING

One who does not know where one stands, stands nowhere. . . .
You can't learn from others unless you learn first who and what you are.
Only teenagers, and shallow ones at that, may be excused for turning against
all that has shaped them. . . . Openness does not mean emptiness.
ANDREW GREELEY

Men do not stand, one by one, like bottles in the rain,
rather like interflowing streams, they share their fortunes.
HARRY EMERSON FOSDICK

SOME OF THE MOST PROFOUND theological questions I have ever seen have come directly from teenagers. To name just a few, in the past year alone I have been asked:

"How could God love my family and allow my mom to be so sick?"

"How can I understand God as my 'father' when my dad died when I was three?"

"What would God think about my dating someone at school who is a different color than I am?"

"Does God care about poverty in India, Haiti or anywhere for that matter? The fighting in Iraq or Kenya?"

"How can Jesus be God if he prays to his Father on the cross?"

"How do I honor both my ethnic heritage and Christian traditions?"

"If God says he wants us to have an abundant life, why can't my parents afford rent even though they work so hard?"

These are just a few of the seemingly never-ending topics I discuss with what are typical teens: they laugh, like to play, have friends in trouble and are seeking a place to grow up as individuals but not isolated. Their lives are filled with real questions. They wonder about the meaning of life and what happens after death. They long for connection here and now but look for hope in the future. If I offer an anemic response, they know it.

I try to anticipate some of their questions based on what I know of adolescent development and culture. While I get it sometimes, they let me know when they need more. "I don't know, but I will try to find the best answer I can" has become a common refrain. All of this is informed by a deep respect for theology and for my students.

Theology and a relationship with Jesus is what sets youth ministers apart from those working with teens purely for secular reasons. While both groups are needed, pastors have a unique and needed voice speaking into the lives of teenagers. Theology is a very human undertaking that seeks to be conceptually adequate to its object of knowledge— nothing less than the mystery of God in Jesus Christ. This incomplete expression of the mystery is always one of the languages in the bilingual pursuit of practical theology; it is, in fact, a key element to practical theology itself, which "takes the insights and resources of the Christian religious tradition of belief and practice, such as the Bible, theology and liturgy, as primary resources for its understandings and activity . . . [and] aims to make a contribution to Christian theology and understanding."[1] Theology is then one of the mandatory languages in the bilingual conversation of practical theology.

---

[1]James Woodward and Stephen Pattison, eds., *The Blackwell Reader in Pastoral and Practical Theology* (Oxford: Blackwell, 2000), p. 8.

The framework of my thinking here comes from James Wm. Mc-Clendon's categorical imperatives, while the writings of Walter Rauschenbusch and Stanley Grenz have helped to flesh out these categories and lead to a full-bodied theology. Returning to McClendon's nuance of Wittgenstein's analogy of a rope, three unique but intertwined strands—and taking cues from both theology and adolescent development—the individual, the communal and the eternal are each unique in function and essence but inseparable from the whole, none deserving pride of place over the other two.[2]

Before moving on to a closer look at the theologians, a better understanding of the rope is needed.

THREE STRANDS, ONE ROPE

Each situation or action in our individual life is constantly influencing and being influenced by our communal experience and eternal context. Teenagers don't always see it this way, but the way they live as individuals is both reflective of and influential toward their community—both local and global. The eternal strand similarly assumes (and requires) the presence of God, whether acknowledged or not. Life is composed of an ongoing chain of situations or actions, the outworking of this interaction of the three strands.

God's work of reconciliation is particularly present within the eternal strand. We read of it in 2 Corinthians:

Therefore, knowing the fear of the Lord, we try to persuade others; but we ourselves are well known to God, and I hope that we also are well known to your consciences. We are not commending ourselves to you again, but giving you an opportunity to boast about us, so that you may be able to answer those who boast in outward appearance and not in the heart. For if we are beside ourselves, it is for God; if we are in our right mind, it is for you. For the love of Christ urges us on, because we are convinced that

---

[2]I use the language of Stanley Grenz in *Theology for the Community of God* as applied to McClendon, concepts which are also present in Rauschenbusch in his writings spanning from 1914-1968. Refer back to chapter two, on adolescent development.

one has died for all; therefore all have died. And he died for all, so that those who live might live no longer for themselves, but for him who died and was raised for them.

From now on, therefore, we regard no one from a human point of view; even though we once knew Christ from a human point of view, we know him no longer in that way. So if anyone is in Christ, there is a new creation: everything old has passed away; see, everything has become new! All this is from God, who reconciled us to himself through Christ, and has given us the ministry of reconciliation; that is, in Christ God was reconciling the world to himself, not counting their trespasses against them, and entrusting the message of reconciliation to us. So we are ambassadors for Christ, since God is making his appeal through us; we entreat you on behalf of Christ, be reconciled to God. For our sake he made him to be sin who knew no sin, so that in him we might become the righteousness of God. (2 Corinthians 5:11-21 NRSV)

This work of reconciliation occurs in many ways and on many levels, all with the same ultimate objective. We may be reconciled as individuals, but never in complete isolation or independence from the community and certainly not eternality. Reconsidering the adaptation of Don Browning's two questions into one (How do I best allow God to work through me to bring about reconciliation? [see p. 38]), then, a closer look at reconciliation is required. We can do this by taking a closer look at three influential theologians.

KINGDOM: WALTER RAUSCHENBUSCH

As an evangelist, Walter Rauschenbusch longed for all to know Christ. As a Christian, he longed for all who know Christ to imitate him and transform their very world. He thought this transformative role is where Christians could most faithfully fulfill their calling from God.

O God, thou great Redeemer of mankind, our hearts are tender in the thought of thee, for in all the afflictions of our race thou hast been afflicted, and in the sufferings of thy people it was thy body that was crucified. Thou hast been wounded by our transgressions and bruised by our iniquities, and all our sins are laid at last on thee. Amid the groaning of creation we behold thy spirit in travail till the sons of God shall be born in freedom and holiness.

We pray thee, O Lord, for the graces of a pure and holy life that we may no longer add to the dark weight of the world's sin that is laid upon thee, but may share with thee in thy redemptive work. As we have thirsted with evil passions to the destruction of men, do thou fill us now with hunger and thirst for justice that we may bear glad tiding to the poor and set at liberty all who are in the prison-house of want and sin. Lay thy Spirit upon us and inspire us with a passion of Christlike love that we may join our lives to the weak and oppressed and may strengthen their cause by bearing their sorrows. And if the evil that is threatened turns to smite us and if we must learn the dark malignity of sinful power, comfort us by the thought that thus we are bearing in our body the marks of Jesus, and that only those who share in his free sacrifice shall feel the plenitude of thy life. Help us in patience to carry forward the eternal cross of the Christ, counting it joy if we, too, are sown as grains of wheat in the furrows of the world, for only by the agony of the righteous comes redemption.[3]

As Rauschenbusch understood it, there had been a shifting of the conception of the meaning of Christianity. "The Bible and all past history speak a new and living language."[4] He sought to teach this new language of the Bible and history to people concerned with the new modern concepts and draw them back to prayer. His final prayer in the same volume expresses his own awareness that he would be misunderstood, misrepresented and mistaken.

O Thou who art the light of my soul, I thank Thee for the incomparable joy of listening to thy voice within, and I know that no

---

[3]Walter Rauschenbusch, *Prayers of the Social Awakening* (Boston: Jordan and More, 1925), pp. 132-33. Rauschenbusch wrote the book as an attempt to "blaze new paths to God for the feet of modern men" (p. 11).
[4]Ibid., p. 9.

word of thine shall return void, however brokenly uttered. If aught in this book was said through lack of knowledge, or through weakness of faith in Thee or of love for men, I pray Thee to over-rule my sin and turn aside its force before it harm thy cause. Pardon the frailty of thy servant, and look upon him only as he sinks his life in Jesus, his Master and Saviour. Amen.[5]

While Rauschenbusch does not employ the term *reconciliation*, the marks of harmony and compatibility with Christ are replete in his writings. He held many strong convictions, none of which excluded personal salvation. Rather, he wished to serve as a corrective for areas which had long been neglected (or worse, created) by the Christian elite. Repeatedly in his writings, Rauschenbusch reminds his audience he is not going to explain his position or understanding of Jesus but that he will discuss the message of Jesus—what Jesus wants for us individually and collectively.[6] This very quest is what led to his emphasis on the communal, and ultimately his emphasis on the kingdom of God.[7] Rauschenbusch viewed the kingdom of God not only in eschatological terms (though definitely not to the exclusion of that view) but also in its potential existence in the present moment through the fulfilling work of Christ and power of the Holy Spirit.

The kingdom of God permeates nearly every writing of Rauschen-

---

[5]Ibid., p. 154.

[6]"It cannot be our task here to discuss the nature of Christ or to attempt to exhaust the eternal significance of his work. We have simply to state the historical fact that Jesus Christ is the prime force in the Christian revolution, and to make clear to ourselves the ways by which his force was exerted and still is exerted to change human society." Walter Rauschenbusch, *The Righteousness of the Kingdom* (New York: Abingdon, 1968), p. 118.

[7]"The kingdom of God" seems to become more and more of an elusive term as theology progresses. Rauschenbusch was clearly influenced by Albrecht Ritschl in believing the kingdom could be present through and within community. While Rauschenbusch predates much of the twentieth-century discussion, rumblings of Bultmann's existential interpretation may be read into the work. See Rudolf Bultmann, *Jesus Christ and Mythology* (New York: Charles Scribner's Sons, 1958), p. 14. Jürgen Moltmann offers a later critique of Bultmann, recovering eschatology as future hope. See Jürgen Moltmann, *The Experiment Hope*, translated by M. Douglas Meeks (Philadelphia: Fortress, 1975), p. 45.

busch's on record.[8] He was one of the only ones (and certainly among the best known) from his time to look around his community and ask why and how the gospel fits into this world. He was using cultural analysis and life experience not to mold the gospel to his own wishes but to work through a way to best communicate the truth of the gospel in his setting. This contextualizing was not normal practice or even a discussion for several more decades. His view—that communication of the gospel came not simply through words or token acts of charity but large-scale sweeping reform of corrupt and oppressive systems—was a radical shift.

Rauschenbusch did not come to his understandings simply through scholarship, as some may think. In fact they are a mosaic of centuries of influence, funneled through his father, August Rauschenbusch; his schooling; his seasons abroad as a child; and his sabbatical while pastoring. While best known for his involvement with social ethics, it was his experience with and influence of pietism that helped shape much of who he was and how he approached the struggles of life.[9] Much of this pietistic influence came through his father and included at least the following elements:

- a rejection of the ecclesiastical status quo in the state churches of Germany

- a rejection of rationalism in favor of pietism

- a missionary assignment in America that culminated in membership in a pietistic denomination—the German Baptists of North America)

---

[8]It is important to remember that Rauschenbusch pastored for ten years and viewed himself as a pastor and evangelist first. After a one-year sabbatical from the pastorate, his public declaration of the kingdom intensified. It was after this time that he published his first work, *Christianity and the Social Crisis*. Were it not for the radical break of this book and the reactions to the first public hearings of his thoughts, we may not know of Rauschenbusch today.

[9]"Pietism was a distinct movement, starting in Germany in the seventeenth century and subsequently exerting great power in England and America. It rejected orthodox Lutheran formalism in favour of a personal, devotional, subjective, individualistic, conversionist pattern of Christianity." Donovan Smucker, *The Origins of Walter Rauschenbusch's Social Ethics* (Buffalo: McGill-Queen's University Press, 1994), p. 21.

- a partial rejection of confessional dogmatism in favor of conscious conversion

- a critical posture toward the world "expressed through a life of personal purity, a network of welfare institutions and schools, and selected social issues."[10]

Within pietism "a limited amount of welfare work may be done for the victims of social tragedy, but it is considered of secondary importance to saving people's souls."[11] Some would say that this emphasis was a point of departure for Walter Rauschenbusch, but in reality he "imbibed from his family a profound personal piety, [along with] a love of learning, a sympathy for the oppressed and a sense of mission."[12]

While beginning his seminary career at Rochester Theological Seminary, Walter was required to take some courses at the University of Rochester (to fill in some gaps from his studies in Germany). He began seeking to understand biblical studies with more up-to-date methods than what archaeology and Hebrew grammar could offer.[13] From his perspective

> the old theology is essentially the theology of the Reformation. The formal principle of the Reformation was: the Bible; its material principles; justification by faith. That is to say: it took its guidance from the Bible and had for its objective personal salvation. But back of the Bible lies the Holy Spirit which inspired it; back of the individual to be saved lies humanity of which he is a part. The formal principle of the new gospel must be the holy Spirit; the material principle must be the Kingdom of God. Thus we shall not go back to Paul alone who inspired the Reformation, but to Jesus Christ, who founded Christianity by preaching the Kingdom of God in the power of the Spirit.[14]

---

[10]Ibid., p. 25.
[11]Ibid., p. 26.
[12]Max Stackhouse, "Rauschenbusch Today: The Legacy of a Loving Prophet," *Christian Century*, January 25, 1989, p. 76.
[13]Paul Minus, *Walter Rauschenbusch: American Reformer* (New York: Macmillan, 1988), p. 39.
[14]Smucker, *Origins of Walter Rauschenbusch's Social Ethics*, p. 434.

Rauschenbusch was not alone in his thinking. There was a movement in the United States and Europe that believed the time had come for a change. It was about this time that Walter had "another soul 'shake-up' which was akin to his conversion and which gave depth to the earlier experience. . . . He 'wished to preach and save souls' and to do hard work for God. He resolved to live literally by the teachings and spirit of Jesus."[15] After graduating, he moved on to pastor for over a decade in New York's Hell's Kitchen.

Due to frustrations over his failing hearing, Walter decided the only thing he could do in fairness to his congregation in New York was to resign. The church leaders responded quickly, offering a one-year sabbatical with pay. Touched by their affection, Rauschenbusch accepted the offer and chose to go to Europe in 1891. It was on this trip that the previously secondhand influence of the Anabaptists took a more central position.[16] Walter spent time in Munich with German historian Ludwig Keller and read the writings of Leopold von Ranke, whose understanding of the difference between Luther and the Anabaptists resonated with Rauschenbusch: "[Luther] said the gospel was to free the soul and not the body. They [the Anabaptists] said, both."[17]

In the Anabaptists, Rauschenbusch found a group of believers interested in freeing not only the soul but also the body, interested in not only the individual but in the community surrounding the individual and eventually the world in which that individual lived. Anabaptists were looking for a return to Christ. In his own notes during this study time in Europe, Rauschenbusch writes that "the Reformation went back of the church to Augustine and Paul. We must go back of Paul to Christ."[18] This was the method of Rauschenbusch, to go back to Jesus for both individual and communal understandings of who we are to be

---

[15]Dores Robinson Sharpe, *Walter Rauschenbusch* (New York: Macmillan, 1942), p. 57.

[16]Smucker, *Origins of Walter Rauschenbusch's Social Ethics*, p. 10. August Rauschenbusch had spent a great deal of time studying the Anabaptist movement.

[17]Minus, *Walter Rauschenbusch*, pp. 69-70, 82.

[18]Ibid., p. 82. While Rauschenbusch's public affirmation of Anabaptists would not occur for two more years, his diary of 1888-1891 shows his admiration and offers insight into the lasting impression they made on his thoughts.

as Christians within the eternal (the kingdom of God)—to restore Christ in every place, in every position, in every corner of the world.[19]

Rauschenbusch's understanding of the kingdom of God was placed in history.[20] He stressed the transforming effect of the church on culture and rejected any hint of withdrawal or the cloistered life.[21] The vast difference with his contemporaries and still today is that he was not content to leave faith with the individual. This came from his own experience and was solidified as he studied Scripture and the teachings and actions of Jesus. From his earliest publication we read:

> Because Jesus believed in the organic growth of the new society, he patiently fostered its growth, cell by cell. Every human life brought under the control of the new spirit which he himself embodied and revealed was an advance of the Kingdom of God. . . . Thus Jesus worked on individuals and through individuals, but His real end was not individualistic, but social, and in His method he employed strong forces.[22]

In a later publication Rauschenbusch writes that "a man is a Christian in the degree in which he shares the spirit and consciousness of Jesus Christ, conceiving God as Jesus knew Him and seeing human life as Jesus realized it."[23] He stated also that "the Kingdom of God is the highest good. The idea of God is the highest and most comprehensive conception in philosophy; the idea of the Kingdom of God is the high-

---

[19]German Baptists were a part of the Northern Baptist Alliance, primarily composed of General (as opposed to Particular) Baptists and Regular (as opposed to Separate) Baptists. Taking these two influences, Rauschenbusch inherited a church legacy which believed in dealing with individual sin, rejected Calvinism (including total depravity), and rejected emotionalism in favor of seeking authentic community by the work of the Holy Spirit through Scripture and the education of the day. Historically, Baptists on any and all sides were for the working class. H. Leon McBeth, *The Baptist Heritage* (Nashville: Broadman Press, 1987), pp. 73, 204.

[20]For more see Stanley Grenz and John R. Franke, eds., *Beyond Foundationalism: Shaping Theology in a Postmodern Context* (Louisville, Ky.: Westminster John Knox, 2001), pp. 239-73.

[21]Smucker, *Origins of Walter Rauschenbusch's Social Ethics*, p. 30.

[22]Rauschenbusch, *Christianity and the Social Crisis*, p. 60.

[23]Walter Rauschenbusch, *Dare We Be Christians?* (Cleveland: Pilgrim Press, 1993), p. 43.

est and broadest idea in sociology and ethics."[24] Everything he writes links Jesus with the larger world. Individuals, for Rauschenbusch, cannot be conceived of apart from the world. The world cannot be conceived apart from God and the role of Christ. In this thought alone the three-strand rope may be identified.

Statements such as, "The institutions of the church, its activities, its worship, and its theology must in the long run be tested by its effectiveness in creating the Kingdom of God,"[25] flow naturally from Rauschenbusch's assumption that professing Christians have a baseline belief and do not need to be persuaded of individual salvation, but in isolation the meaning of such statements can be greatly skewed. So Rauschenbusch offers further clarification elsewhere:

> Individualistic theology sees everywhere countless sinful individuals who must all go through the same process of repentance, faith, justification, and regeneration, and who in due time die and go to heaven or hell. . . . The social gospel tries to see the progress of the Kingdom of God in the flow of history. . . . Its chief interest is the Kingdom of God; and the Kingdom of God is history seen in a religious and teleological way.[26]

Rauschenbusch further clarifies his position in his last writing. "The Kingdom of God is humanity organized according to the will of God."[27] The kingdom plays a crucial role as it is "always coming, always pressing in on the present, always big with possibility and always inviting immediate action."[28] It is evident in the decade between his writings that Rauschenbusch learned to listen to his critics and more clearly state his understanding of God's role in the individual life while losing none of his fervor for what he believed about the connection to the kingdom. In his better-known publications (*Christianity and the Social*

---

[24]Walter Rauschenbusch, *The Social Principles of Jesus* (New York: Gorsett and Dunlap, 1916), p. 59.

[25]Ibid., p. 143.

[26]Ibid., p. 146.

[27]Walter Rauschenbusch, *A Theology for the Social Gospel* (New York: Macmillan, 1918), p. 142.

[28]Ibid., p. 141.

Crisis and *A Theology for the Social Gospel*) Rauschenbusch seems to assume at least a Lutheran understanding of the gospel; in his call for a nuanced, Anabaptist understanding he is neither negating nor denying the former but rather simply assuming an audience who already accepts and understands individual salvation. This is clearly evident when he states, "There is no man within the domain of Christendom who has not been influenced by Christ in some way."[29] The question becomes what Rauschenbusch considers to be Christendom. Following the pattern of previous writings, it is the kingdom, which is to be realized (as best as possible) both in the here and now, and in the eschaton.

Even with his prolific writings teeming with thoughts on the kingdom, Rauschenbusch firmly believes in a personal relationship with Christ.

> The salvation of the individual is of course, an essential part of salvation. Every new being is a new problem of salvation. It is always a great and wonderful thing when a young spirit enters into voluntary obedience to God and feels the higher freedom with which Christ makes us free. It is one of the miracles of life. The burden of the individual is as heavy now as ever.[30]

His struggle came in feeling like this relationship had been belittled by the practice of his day. "Things have been simmered down to signing a card, shaking hands, or being introduced to the evangelist. . . . It is time to overhaul our understanding of the kind of change we hope to produce by personal conversion and regeneration."[31] The concern of Rauschenbusch was equally for the reconciliation of the individual and for the transformation that would take place both within the individual and as they live in community and within the eternal realm of God. His emphasis was captured posthumously in writings where he confessed, "He [Jesus] taught that every man was personally responsible for

---

[29]Rauschenbusch, *Dare We Be Christians?* p. 44.
[30]Rauschenbusch, *Theology for the Social Gospel*, p. 95. It is interesting to note that the further along Rauschenbusch went in life, the more he was accused of allowing the kingdom to supersede individual needs.
[31]Ibid., p. 97.

his acceptance of the Messianic salvation. It would not come to all alike. . . . Christ taught the forgiveness of sins for the individual soul."[32]

Critiqued for his lack of emphasis on traditional salvific notions, nevertheless, they were never absent. Dores Sharpe recalls a private conversation with Walter:

> Rather abruptly he turned his steady penetrating gaze on me and asked: "How do you think of me and my work?" My reply was: "I think of you as an evangelist and of your work as evangelism of the truest sort." The effect was electric for he threw his arms around me and, with deep emotion said: "I have always wanted to be thought of in that way."[33]

Rauschenbusch was misunderstood by many. This is not to say there is no recognition of the prevalent misgivings that the teaching of the social gospel have created over the last century. What was robust with Christology too often was diluted to at best secular social work and at worst, tax breaks for those seeking a charity in the name of philanthropy. Rauschenbusch was first and foremost an evangelist, always seeking to find his role in how the Holy Spirit could best use him to help reconcile individuals to God and to help reconcile the community to God. Concerned for the individual but equally for the communal, he embraced this tension as the reconciling role of Christ.

COMMUNITY: STANLEY J. GRENZ

Removed by more than a lifetime from Rauschenbusch, Stanley Grenz proposes a distinctly communal perspective on theology. While never mentioning Rauschenbusch in any writings, the similarities of influence make these two theologians highly compatible. Each declares the designation *evangelical* as part of their identity. Unlike Rauschenbusch, however, Grenz is acutely aware of the influences in his life.

> Stating the matter simply, "community" is central to my theological thinking because I am convinced that it is both at the heart of

---

[32]Walter Rauschenbusch, *Righteousness of the Kingdom*, p. 96.
[33]Sharpe, *Walter Rauschenbusch*, p. 393.

the biblical narrative and speaks clearly to the contemporary context. More specifically, I would add that community is crucial because it arises out of the very essence of God. At the heart of Christian theology is the doctrine of the Trinity, which declares that God is not only the one who enters into relationship with creation, and hence relates to us in time. Rather, God is internally relational within the Godhead, and hence eternally relational. Moreover, the Christian teaching declares that God suggests that mere one-to-one relationship does not exhaust the essence of God. Instead, the one God of the Bible is the fellowship of the Father, Son and Holy Spirit, to cite traditional Trinitarian terminology. In short, the God revealed in Jesus is communal or community.[34]

Raised the son of a Baptist minister in a conference having its roots in work with German immigrants, Grenz was shaped for life by

the warm-hearted pietism that characterized the early leaders, many of whom had come out of German Lutheran Pietism. This group never participated in modernist-fundamentalist controversy. . . . They were held together by the warm-hearted approach to the faith and the relationality they sensed within the group.

Grenz's academic training steered him toward a "more cognitive approach to the faith and consequently to theology as an intellectual discipline," but he remained strongly linked to "the pietism of my upbringing." A seminal moment came in the late 1980s.

I read Robert Bellah's intriguing study *Habits of the Heart*, on the effects of radical individualism in American culture, and I returned to Munich to write a book on theology of my Doktorvater, Wolfhart Pannenberg. The result was an awareness that something was missing in the "scholastic" approach to theology: true

---

[34]Stanley Grenz, "Community and Relationships: A Theological Take," *Talk: The Mainstream Magazine*, February 9, 2003 <www.stanleyjgrenz.com/articles/talk_mag.html>. See also Stanley Grenz, *Theology for the Community of God* (Nashville: Broadman & Holman, 1994), p. x.

piety. Upon my return to the USA, where I was teaching at the time, I set out to rewrite my theological lectures in a manner that would incorporate into the foundational work that I had already done, the pietist aspect in a manner that gave place to the importance of corporate relationality, i.e., community.[35]

This dual influence is evident throughout his work.[36] This influence was so strong that Grenz wrote *Theology for the Community of God,* in which he states on the first page of the preface that "my goal is to consider faith within the context of God's central program for creation, namely, the establishment of community."[37] On the surface and even glancing through the table of contents, this looks much like any other text on systematic theology. Within its pages, however, Grenz crafts a distinct look at Christian doctrine always in relation to community.

Reconciliation fulfills what Grenz considers God's ultimate goal, community.

> God is throughout eternity the community of the Father, Son and Spirit. In history, therefore, the triune God is at work seeking to bring creation into participation in this eternal fellowship. . . . Understood in this manner, . . . Christian anthropology sets forth the glorious truth that humans are created in the divine image, a concept best understood in a corporate or community sense. Although created for community, because of the fall humans are estranged from themselves, from each other, from their environment, and—most tragically of all—from God. Yet the Christian story does not end on the negative note. Humans are also objects of God's reconciling work.[38]

---

[35]Grenz, "Community and Relationships." *Habits of the Heart* contains a lengthy discussions on both the concepts of community and individuality. See their brief glossary definitions in Robert N. Bellah, Richard Masden, William Sullivan, Ann Swindler and Steven Tipton, *Habits of the Heart: Individualism and Commitment in American Life* (Los Angeles: University of California Press, 1996), pp. 333-34.

[36]Grenz's dual emphasis on piety and scholastic theology is most clear in his "Concerns of a Pietist with a PhD," paper presented November 23, 2002, at the American Academy of Religion, Toronto.

[37]Grenz, *Theology for the Community of God,* p. ix.

[38]Ibid., p. 316.

The preparation for reconciliation is present from the time of creation. When reconciliation occurs, community is restored in its entirety—human beings restored with one another, with the environment and, most magnificently, with God—thus fulfilling "the deepest intentions of God in creation."[39]

Our human understanding of how to live this out is found in our very human undertaking of the study of God, or theology. At the risk of erring on the side of community within reconciliation, Grenz accepts Catherine Mowry LaCugna's "inseparability of theology (proper) and soteriology"[40] to contend that theology builds from the experience of salvation, the reconciliation of the individual. LaCugna sees this experience as revealing the "mystery of God" which is "the mystery of persons in communion."[41] Grenz affirms her view that in salvation "'we become by grace what God is by nature,' namely, persons in full communion with God and with every creature."[42] As God is at work and humans individually experience his reconciliation, they also exist as individuals in relation to others; consequently reconciliation with others will occur. An individual's imitation of Christ in the work of reconciliation in this world is a natural result of the experiential work of God being reconciled to the individual. Just as theology is inseparable from salvation, this theology is descriptive of the effect of soteriology. In the one act of the reconciling work of God, the individual is brought into eternal community.

Our experience of reconciliation sets the expectation for responsive action. We participate in community through acts of commitment: "Our raison d'etre is to glorify God by walking together as a community and thereby reflecting the character of the Triune God, who is love."[43] In other words, the pietistic character is not to be cloistered and

[39]Grenz and Franke, *Beyond Foundationalism*, p. 202.
[40]Stanley Grenz, *The Social God and the Relational Self: A Trinitarian Theology of the Imago Dei* (Louisville, Ky.: Westminster John Knox, 2001), pp. 53-54.
[41]Catherine Mowry LaCugna, *God for Us: The Trinity and Christian Life* (San Francisco: HarperSanFrancisco, 1992), p. 1.
[42]Ibid.
[43]Stanley Grenz, *Created for Community: Connecting Christian Belief with Christian Living* (Grand Rapids: Baker, 1998), p. 234.

hidden away like a well-guarded secret tryst with God but is to be celebrated through daily expression in transformative acts of commitment. God is intimately involved in the affairs of our individual lives and the world at large. As those who have experienced reconciliation, it is our privilege to have God work through us in order that we may join him in his work. Feeding the hungry, taking time to listen to the lonely, creating a beautiful work of art, seeking justice and peace—these are all natural outpourings of the responses we may offer as a result of our relationship with God. This is not what earns or seals the relationship; the absence of any such response, however, invites the question of whether a relationship is indeed present. "God's reign—God's will—is reconciliation and fellowship."[44]

Grenz is concerned with maintaining a right doctrine at all times. His piety has never compromised his cognitive tendency.

> My commitment to warm-heartedness is evident in my repeated declarations that the *sine qua non* of evangelicalism is not primarily doctrinal uniformity, but a particular spirituality. At the same time, I bristle when some pietistic evangelicals use the warm-heartedness as a pretense for anti-intellectual, anti-theological bias that glorifies "simple believing" and vilifies any attempt to grapple with the intellectual dimension of the faith. In such a climate, I link arms with those who call themselves "confessing evangelicals," for I am deeply concerned that the Christian church maintain its doctrinal integrity in the face of sloppy theology and the inroads of heterodoxy. Like the "confessing evangelicals," I am aware that a theologically naïve "experientialism" can produce a theologically-vacuous "spirituality," and so I share their fervor in combating this debilitating tendency. Moreover, being convinced that theological conviction is a crucial well-spring of Christian living, I affirm the importance of sound theology for the on-going health and vitality of the church, and I seek to model my own life and foster the lives of others a theologically-tuned and theologically in-tune discipleship."[45]

---

[44]Ibid., p. 257.
[45]Grenz, "Concerns of a Pietist with a PhD."

While he would not use this language, Grenz comes across as a modified practical theologian, believing that "every experience is necessarily tied to an understanding of reality, an interpretive framework, that both facilitates it and emerges from it."[46] He cautions about the use of the word *experience*, wanting to be clear that the church's communal reflection of biblical truth, not any individual experience, is formative of theology.[47]

It is possible to be pietistic and not evangelical. Grenz's "strong regard for doctrine arises as a crucial and necessary by-product of my being an evangelical committed to the gospel of heartfelt transformation."[48] His strong evangelical nature has been honed over years within a tradition that takes seriously the salvation of the individual while realizing we were neither created to remain isolated nor are allowed to remain pietistically aloof once reconciliation has occurred if right doctrine is to adhere.

Eternity is represented explicitly within the writings and thoughts of Grenz and implicitly through his understanding of the communal Trinity. Grenz views the eternal (third strand) or eschatological as intrinsically linked to pragmatic issues within theology.

I think that the proper perspective from which to engage in theological reflection and construction is the future or eschatological viewpoint. . . . We should be seeking to answer central theological questions from the perspective of the eschatological fullness of God's program for the universe. Hence, we should define what it means to be human from the destiny that God intends for us. As Christians, we know this destiny to be that of our being risen and glorified saints enjoying fellowship with God throughout eternity. Similarly, we should define the church from the vantage point of our communal purpose to be the sign and foretaste of the fullness of community that will be ours when Christ returns. Therefore, we must see ourselves as called to seek to live in the

[46]Ibid.
[47]Stanley J. Grenz, *Revisioning Evangelical Theology: A Fresh Agenda for the 21st Century* (Downers Grove, Ill.: InterVarsity Press, 1993), pp. 91-94.
[48]Grenz, "Concerns of a Pietist with a PhD."

present in the light of the glorious future that awaits us. But the valid orientation toward the future ought not to lead us to cut ourselves off from the past. As many sociological theorists have pointed out, a true community is a "community of hope" (one that anticipates its glorious future) as well as a community of memory, i.e., a people who remember their communal past.[49]

Grenz would say it is important for the church to tell its story in terms relevant to contemporary culture, but he is careful to pay heed to the future and past alike. He sees Jesus as the Revealer, Effector and Originator in the divine program of establishing community. "Our Lord stands at the beginning of a new fellowship of humans, forming its foundation and fountainhead. The new corporate reality Jesus inaugurates is the church, the company who pioneer the eschatological community of God."[50]

In even simpler terms, Grenz observes from the Bible that "God's purposes go beyond our individual existence or even the human story. The divine goal is ultimately cosmic in scope."[51] Eschatology carries with it the sense of hope for the future—not as a generic hope for all but a hope as God, the Creator, addresses each individually to be drawn into community.

Consequently our understanding of community will always be particular never generic. Indeed a nonfoundationalist theological method will be the outworking of the particular, because it eschews the generically human to articulate, reflect on, and explicate the beliefs of a specific faith community. Hence, Christian theology will be concerned with and formed by the particularly Christian understanding of community.[52]

He understands that "the ultimate purpose of theology is to speak

---

[49]Grenz, "Community and Relationships." Notice the very specific wording years after his initial reading of *Habits of the Heart* to express an understanding of community, in particular a "community of memory."

[50]Grenz, *Theology for the Community of God*, p. 459.

[51]Grenz, *Created for Community*, pp. 275-76. See also Grenz, *Revisioning Evangelical Theology*, p. 98.

[52]Grenz and Franke, *Beyond Foundationalism*, p. 229.

about the actual world for the sake of the mission of the church of the present, anticipatory era. And for this to occur, theology must be oriented toward the future; it must be eschatological."[53] We are reconciled and enter into a community that is for eternity.

EXPERIENCE: JAMES WM. MCCLENDON JR.

Baptist thinking is known as "a mélange of data of mixed or unknown value, so that an important part of the theologian's task is to discover the community's formative convictions before trying to interpret them and then to restate them for the future."[54] James McClendon Jr. fits this pattern of discovery-interpretation-restatement perfectly. He defines theology as

> the discovery, understanding, and transformation of the convictions of a convictional community, including the discovery and critical revision of their relation to one another and to whatever else there is.[55]

The explication of this definition of theology consumes (in one way or another) three volumes of McClendon's work, spanning fifteen years by publication dates (many more by the years of thought and preliminary work). For McClendon, discovery and understanding point to "what theologians do in homage to what is handed on to them, but in 'transformation' [the definition] points to what is necessarily creative in their task. Theology is thus both a descriptive discipline and a normative one."[56] This concept is a basic premise upon which this work is built; theology consisting of reflective discovery, understanding and transformation, in his mind, is the Baptist way.

I felt in over my head when I first entered the nascent field of practical theology, in part because the water I found myself swimming in was

[53]Ibid., p. 273.
[54]Curtis Freeman, James Wm. McClendon Jr. and C. Rosalee Velloso da Silva, *Baptist Roots: A Reader in the Theology of a Christian People* (Valley Forge, Penn.: Judson Press, 1999), p. 2.
[55]James Wm. McClendon Jr., *Systematic Theology*, vol. 1, *Ethics* (Nashville: Abingdon, 1986), p. 23.
[56]Ibid.

being described only after the fact. Points of influence are much more easily identified in hindsight. McClendon is a leader in that regard, giving credence to the "idea of 'experience' under the heading of narrative."

> "Experience" is a systematically ambiguous word, referring now to evanescent, private, inward feeling, and again to matters of communal and public knowledge. If, however, we see that the experience that matters for the Christian life is not mere flashes of feeling, but is what we have lived through and lived out in company with one another, the experience that constitutes our share in the Christ story, . . . experience in that sense is the enduring or timely aspect of our lives in relation to God and one another; as plot and character in some setting, it is the stuff of narrative. Every theology is linked to some narrative; successful theology, knowing this, discovers and renovates its own narrative base.[57]

We come to this communal or "connecting" narrative with our own stories. From crucial decisions to silly mistakes, they are value-laden; and though often presented in thin ways, the reality of their thickness is ever present. Ethics—the "stuff" of our personal narratives (the characters, plots and settings of our daily activities)—is what McClendon chooses as the point of commencement for his three-part offering in systematic theology.[58]

Among many profound reasons McClendon offers for beginning his work with ethics, one is the most compelling of all. "When the study of systematic theology is understood as preparation for ministry, there is little reason to initiate students to it via that part of systematic theology most abstruse, most remote from daily life, and therefore least congenial. Many students, starting there, quit as soon as they can!"[59] Ethics,

---

[57]Ibid., pp. 38-39.

[58]For McClendon ethics was not solely a classroom exercise. It "is the study (or systematization) of morals, while 'morals' (or 'morality') means the actual conduct of people viewed with concern for right and wrong, good and evil, virtue and vice." Ibid., p. 47. Ethics does offer theories of conduct but has the conduct, the action, as its focus. One cannot simply have good theory and be considered to have mastered ethics; it is in the practice of such theory that ethics takes place in its fullness.

[59]Ibid., p. 42.

then, is not an umbrella term, nor a logical or ontological priority, but a chronological priority.

> Theology does not simply serve itself but should make a difference in Christian life. Christian doctrine ought to help clarify the ways in which Christian faith should be lived and provide motivation and encouragement for Christians, individually and corporately, to live in accordance with their commitment. Theology must be related to life and ethics.[60]

Reconciliation within an individual and community is a factor in this approach. "We begin by finding the shape of the common life in the body of Christ, which is for Christians partly a matter of self-discovery."[61] As our identity in Christ is more clearly and deeply comprehended, our ethics (our conduct) palpably reveals this process.[62]

Our identity, or our character, is of utmost importance in looking at ethics. Character is what moves an action from one of whim or selfish motive to one with a positive intent or *telos*. McClendon's understanding of character is not one of independence but of community: "Communities have their own distinctive characters, and . . . signs of this distinctive character are the community's holding certain convictions—the same convictions that inform and give shape to many individual members of the community."[63] The community shapes the individual, recognizing that the individual does not exist alone. Christianity turns on the character of Christ.

As McClendon works through the three strands—the individual, the communal and the eternal—he is convinced that none may stand alone. "God as God is present to us in every strand, every dimension of our existence."[64] He turns to Paul as an example of these three working

---

[60]Grenz and Franke, *Beyond Foundationalism*, p. 18.

[61]McClendon, *Ethics*, p. 45.

[62]By no means is McClendon the only one to assert a commencement in ethics. For further discussion see Stanley Hauerwas, *A Community of Character: Toward a Constructive Christian Ethic* (Notre Dame, Ind.: University of Notre Dame Press, 1981).

[63]James Wm. McClendon Jr. and James M. Smith, *Biography as Theology: How Life Stories Can Remake Theology* (Philadelphia: Trinity Press, 1990), p. 17.

[64]McClendon, *Ethics*, p. 186.

together. Created in the image of God, living in community as modeled in the Trinity with hope grounded in eschatological implications, we too are able to participate with God in all three strands. Through the connecting-narrative, all three are clearly linked.

McClendon was an early voice in the use of narrative for ethics.[65] He sees narrative as that which connects the Bible with experience. Specifically, "the narrative the Bible reflects, the story of Israel, of Jesus, and of the church, is intimately related to the narrative we ourselves live."[66] *Experience* for McClendon is not an ambiguous term referring at will to private or public events and feelings. "Experience that matters for Christian life is not mere flashes of feeling, but is what we have lived through and lived out in company with one another, the experience that constitutes our share in the Christ story. . . . Experience in that sense is the enduring or timely aspect of our lives in relation to God and one another."[67] In the narrative sense, experience has the possibility to be positive or negative.[68] These experiences, whether good or bad, fold into the mystery of God as a "connecting-narrative."

The connecting-narrative provides connectivity for all others. By no means do we as humans have an objective vantage point; rather, narratives are told from a distinct, local perspective. This does not negate the rule of God through eternity, but we are not able, no matter how hard we try, to embrace the totalizing vision of the Enlightenment. Truth cannot be achieved through sheer will or intellectual assent. It would be folly if not heresy to claim the ability to reach equal understanding with God through study or scientific empiricism. It is in the local that authentic narratives are able to exist; they eschew "the generically human for the mosaic of beliefs of a particular faith community."[69] The connecting-narrative hearkens back to a biblical model seen throughout Scripture; it recognizes the Trinity while acknowledging our humanity.

---

[65]Stanley Grenz and Roger Olson, *20th-Century Theology: God and the World in a Transitional Age* (Downers Grove, Ill.: InterVarsity Press, 1992), p. 279.

[66]McClendon, *Ethics*, p. 38.

[67]Ibid., pp. 38-39.

[68]Class notes, "Types of Christian Theology" by James Wm. McClendon Jr., Fuller Theological Seminary, Pasadena, California, February 25, 1999.

[69]Grenz and Franke, *Beyond Foundationalism*, p. 249.

It allows for particularity with humility rather than requiring a modernist universality.

The connecting-narrative seeks to provide a way for all stories, disparate as they may seem, to be connected while still retaining their individuality. Connections will come in a variety of ways, from obvious to distant or even seemingly impossible. At times the connections will seem like a complicated labyrinth of webbing; at other times, it will be a direct line in close proximity. Regardless of the end result, the connecting-narrative is what both constitutes the sum total and creates the connections for all.

THEOLOGICAL MOSAIC

Reconciliation is the work of God in this world. Our job is to figure out how we, through the power of the Holy Spirit, have joined, are joining and will join God in this work. Rauschenbusch, Grenz and McClendon each share common threads, largely expressed through narrative accounts; each emphasizes the communal perspective, though not to the abandonment of the individual. Theology for them is incomplete when relegated to the theoretical and comes into its own only as reflective practice or praxis occurs. Each brings the kingdom of God (the eschatological or eternal realm) into integral daily considerations.

Apart from the imperative of transformative reconciliation, youth ministry would not exist. Adolescent development and cultural issues are well-established, independent disciplines apart from theological considerations. They can only come into their fullness, however, when the reality of God is factored into their existence. Theology offers explanation in otherwise ambiguous aspects of each.

Transformative reconciliation begins with the experience of the individual adolescent moving toward adulthood. When a typical individual adolescent experiences love, a natural response occurs. The experience of love is expressed in community through large and small acts, which themselves can be categorized as powerful acts of justice and mercy. With each encounter of love, justice and mercy, Christ is at work fulfilling his reconciling work in the world.

In this way, no individual in any stage of life is ever through with the transformative power of Christ. The adolescent task, when all goes well, is individuation, but this is only one step in the lifelong process of differentiation. An intentional bilingual conversation between a three-strand theology and other relative disciplines allows youth workers to play an active role in God's work of reconciliation in the life of an adolescent.

QUESTIONS FOR FURTHER THOUGHT

1. Why is it important to consider all three strands of the rope—the individual, communal and eternal? To what extent is each addressed in your ministry?

2. What role does community play within your tradition/church?

3. How can considerations for both the now and not yet be addressed in youth ministry?

4. How can you help teens to seek God's guidance and consider theology when making choices in life?

6

A DEPTH ENCOUNTER
WITH CENTRAL VIRTUES

LOVE, MERCY, JUSTICE AND TRANSFORMATION

And what was it that delighted me? Only this—to love and be loved.

AUGUSTINE

Justice is not a case of the "haves" giving to the "have nots." That is far too unworthy and shallow an interpretation of God's intent for us. We must recognize that all people are our brothers and sisters. . . . We are all members of God's family. We would want the best for our family. . . . It is our responsibility as part of being God's children to actively try to make God's Kingdom come on earth.

DESMOND TUTU

Mercy is only to the undeserving. But such we all are made in the sight of God. . . . Nothing can make injustice just but mercy.

ROBERT FROST

OUR YOUTH GROUP SAT IN silence. We spent a Sunday afternoon huddled into one living room, sitting on every available space to be able to see the screen. Three weeks earlier one of my high school girls had come to me asking if she could lead a discussion for the youth group around the movie *Invisible Children*. She was already a part of Amnesty International at her school and pushed our youth group in the following month to sponsor a child in Ethiopia. Interestingly, this is also the student I have had to discipline in ways I never dreamed would be a part of youth ministry.

Justice is a part of my regular conversation with her, both justice in the world and justice in what she is currently encountering. Our discussions have given birth to wrestling with mercy, and as we then consider Jesus, the connections between love, justice and mercy become both more clear and more complex. She is seeking to extend mercy and justice around the world. What is even more amazing, in recent months she has been seeking to extend mercy and justice in her community and even her home.

A Christocentric practical theology of youth ministry grounds an expression of the three virtues of love, justice and mercy as the transformative power of Christ becomes evident in the life of an adolescent. The relationships of love, justice and mercy are essential as maturing virtues in the lives of all people. Comprehension and application of these virtues is greatly affected by the worldview not only of the one experiencing the virtues but also of those interpreting from the community as well. For the Christian, the transformative power of Christ works with each of these, offering specific models of love, patterns of justice and understandings of mercy. Theological insight into these three arise daily in the lives of adolescents individually, communally and for eternity, as they are traversing the waters from childhood to adulthood.

ADOLESCENT EXPERIENCE

While adolescence offers a specific developmental phase, this movement toward maturation is not a linear progression. Transformation ultimately brings with it the cognitive recognition that something much greater than the passage from childhood to adulthood is being effected. As this is occurring, the journey toward transformation is begun. "Through Christ, God constitutes us individually as believers and corporately as a community of believers."[1] Ideally, the individual adoles-

---

[1]Stanley Grenz and John R. Franke, eds., *Beyond Foundationalism: Shaping Theology in a Postmodern Context* (Louisville, Ky.: Westminster John Knox, 2001), p. 48.

cent works this out in actual relationships of community as he or she encounters circumstances where justice issues occur.

For the adolescent, choices with eternal consequences begin to transpire long before this is recognized. Once acknowledged, the depth of understanding of the self, the other, the community and God continues throughout a lifetime. There are those who never come to a place of having lived deeply or traveled far enough on the journey of transformation to comprehend the eternal ramifications and realities of each stage of the life cycle. The authentic spiritual experience of God initiates the work of reconciliation leading to transformation. This transformation is both intrapersonal and interpersonal reconciliation—for the now and the not yet.

> The Christian vision with its eschatological ontology does not apply only to the human person. Rather, it is cosmic in scope. In fact, ultimately it is directed to a new heaven and a new earth— that is a new cosmos. We, in turn, participate in the eschatological reality insofar as the new creation encompasses redeemed humans.[2]

Reconciliation and transformation are two sides of the same coin. There is an interdependence of the two, allowing either to initiate the other. Where one exists the other is present, often making it difficult if not impossible to know in what chronology. The exploration of the three interlocking virtues within transformation begins with a theological consideration of love.

LOVE

Stanley Grenz identifies love as the fundamental attribute of God. "Because throughout eternity and apart from the world the one God is love, the God who is love cannot but respond to the world in his own eternal essence which is love."[3] This love, within a developmental stage marked by and filled with a sense of loss, negation and negotiation, is

---

[2]Ibid., p. 271.
[3]Stanley Grenz, *Theology for the Community of God* (Nashville: Broadman & Holman, 1994), p. 93.

vital to the individual adolescent as she moves toward adulthood. While it is experienced between the individual and God, this love occurs within a particular social context, location and time.

James McClendon affirms that "love is God's interactive authority at work: God's creative loving evokes the creature's love which (thus evoked) knows that it touches ultimacy."[4] This one statement touches the three strands—individual, communal and eternal—which are essential to authentic humanness. As we experience love as the foundational attribute of God, it elicits a response both temporal (individual and communal) and eternal: transformation and ultimately reconciliation. "The community God is creating is a reconciled people who are concerned about compassion, justice, righteousness, and above all, love."[5]

There is a wide spectrum of human response to the love of God. "We love," 1 John 4:19 informs us, "because he first loved us." Walter Rauschenbusch offers a few possibilities. "Negatively Christian love means abstinence from harm; positively it means the bestowal of good at cost to ourselves."[6] Views of love are as varied as the potential human responses to the love of God. The response may be one of overwhelming gratitude, humility, feelings of unworthiness or confusion. The varieties of responses are seemingly endless.

In traditional theology, *agapē* love has been viewed as (1) benevolence, (2) obedience, (3) sacrifice, (4) mutuality and (5) equal regard. All five of these offer aspects of the nature of love; the last can include all five dimensions within itself and so will here be accepted as normative.[7] *Agapē* in this sense is not a "one size fits all" generic love; it prohibits the discriminatory judgments that could be in place when looking at special traits within an individual. It does not determine whether the person is to be cared about or to be loved at all; rather, it allows and

---

[4]James Wm. McClendon Jr., *Systematic Theology*, vol. 2, *Doctrine* (Nashville: Abingdon, 1994), p. 458.

[5]Grenz, *Theology for the Community of God*, p. 661.

[6]Walter Rauschenbusch, *The Righteousness of the Kingdom* (Nashville: Abingdon, 1968), p. 182.

[7]Gene Outka suggests that love may be viewed in three ways: as equal regard, self-sacrifice and mutuality. See Gene Outka, *Agape: An Ethical Analysis* (New Haven, Conn.: Yale University Press, 1972), pp. 7-43.

requires that she be loved in a way that is unique and appropriate to her, regardless of her ability to return love.[8]

Martin Buber describes this as an "I-Thou relationship":

> The relation to the You is unmediated. Nothing conceptual inter-venes between I and You, no prior knowledge and no imagina-tion. . . . No purpose intervenes between I and You, no greed and no anticipation.[9]

A relationship is formed simply out of equal regard; even seemingly noble gain is not the basis for the relationship.[10] Much earlier, Im-manuel Kant proposed a similar idea: "something whose existence has itself an absolute value. . . . Man, and in general every rational being, exists as an end in himself, not merely as a means for arbitrary use by this or that will."[11]

The love of God is not disinterested in the relationship with an in-dividual (self-sacrifice), nor does it require a mutual response (mutual-ity). Equal regard (which often manifests as neighbor love, the love that occurs in and around you in the world in which you live)[12] is a way to receive love from Christ through others, or to love others as Christ works through individuals.

Adolescents not only want this love (even if they cannot express this directly); they need a truly loving, supportive community which is deeply committed to and interested in who they are as persons and able

---

[8]Ibid., pp. 19-20.

[9]Martin Buber, *I and Thou,* trans. Walter Kaufman (New York: Charles Scribner's Sons, 1970), p. 62.

[10]I am grateful for conversations with Dan Kern around this subject and his reminder of Kant's much earlier work. Kern also suggests a reading of Heidegger for a much deeper and more poetic study. See Martin Heidegger, *Basic Writings,* trans. David F. Krell (San Francisco: Harper and Row, 1977).

[11]Immanuel Kant, *Groundwork of the Metaphysic of Morals,* trans. H. J. Paton (San Francisco: Harper Torchbooks, 1956), p. 95.

[12]A very different perspective and context, yet helpful on a number of levels, is pre-sented by Stephen Post, who considers love and its manifestations in another com-munity of those seemingly difficult to love: those with Alzheimer's disease. Post presents love as forgiveness, compassion, humor, loyalty, creativity, justice, reverence (respect) and attentive listening. Stephen Post, "Love and the Deeply Forgetful," November 2005, Azusa Pacific University, Azusa, California.

to nurture them into the ability to offer equal regard all on their own.

LOVE AND JUSTICE

Neither is love isolated from justice. "The central commandment of the Christian law is love. It excludes all wrong-doing as a matter of course. It demands in addition the relieving of suffering and the bestowing of good to the utmost limit of our strength."[13] Love is not for the faint-hearted or those seeking the easy route. When fully responding to the evocative love of God, the limits of strength will not only be reached but stretched.

By its very nature, love exists between individuals as connections are made and community is built. *Agapē* is "distinguished in self-other relations not so much because of the greater sacrifice it may involve but because of its greater personalism. Only when two people meet each other in openness and affection does agape come fully into its own."[14] Joseph Fletcher brings love and justice into dialogue, seeing the two as "the same, for justice is love distributed, nothing else."[15]

God's love evokes a response, which is worked out in community. A very significant communal manifestation is in our participation in justice. While justice receives much attention in theology, ethics, economics, jurisprudence and related fields both theoretical and applied, youth ministry literature is nearly void of any considerations.[16] The practical need of this concept within the lives of adolescents as individuals, in community and in the world is crucial to their development through the crucial passages in the world of the adolescent.

Justice is a central issue in the maturation of adolescents as they work out their place in association with others.[17] They often use the term

---

[13]Rauschenbusch, *Righteousness of the Kingdom*, p. 186.

[14]Outka, *Agape*, pp. 81-82.

[15]Joseph Fletcher, *Situation Ethics* (Philadelphia: Westminster Press, 1966), p. 87.

[16]A few exceptions include Amy Jacober, "Balance and Justice: A Youth Ministry Perspective," *The Journal of Student Ministries*, 2008; and Kenda Creasy Dean, Chap Clark and Dave Rahn, *Starting Right: Thinking Theologically About Youth Ministry* (Grand Rapids: Zondervan, 2001), p. 251.

[17]For an interesting look at issues of justice and injustice and potential ramifications for children and adolescents, see Jonathan Kozol, *Amazing Grace: The Lives of Children and the Conscience of a Nation* (New York: Perennial, 2000).

justice as equated with *fairness*. They know when a teacher is being just in grading. They know when a friend is not being just after hearing a piece of untrue gossip. More than that, they live within the confines of a society that has created laws which place boundaries on their lives, and they slowly realize they had no say in those laws. Issues of justice appear in all life decisions, from the most mundane to the most complex. Regardless of where they are found, the cumulative effect of justice achieved or injustice endured helps define who they will become and guides them in finding a place and a role within community.

Mercy, meanwhile, is seemingly in opposition to justice. It is most often juxtaposed with justice and seemingly cannot find a voice apart from this relationship. Mercy is not about what society deems as right and prudent, nor about receiving what one merits or deserves. And yet, mercy does seem to have many of the same goals as justice—desiring that the person be honored and relationships restored; desiring that all receive according to their needs, not by what they have earned or merited. Mercy flourishes in relationships where equal regard and justice have occurred. It is the outpouring of the internalization and commingling of love and justice.

Mercy is commonly seen to be more of an individual than communal experience. It is not legislated, as is much justice, and it is barely taught on a macro level as necessary for the healthy formation of a society. Justice tends to be the central demand of a group—for those wronged, for those to whom something is owed, or simply to maintain societal standards. Mercy, on the other hand, is brought up when one witnesses suffering firsthand. Mercy is requested—a desire to see each case considered individually and each consequence made proportionate to the wrongdoing and cognizant of the individual circumstances under which an injustice was committed. Mercy is reacting to someone else's suffering. Jon Sobrino contends that at a basic level, mercy is often motivated by the suffering of individuals in this world.[18] Mercy is an "action, or more precisely a re-action to someone else's suffering, now interiorized

---

[18]Jon Sobrino, *The Principle of Mercy: Taking the Crucified People from the Cross* (Maryknoll, N.Y.: Orbis, 1994), p. 16.

within oneself—a reaction to suffering that has come to penetrate one's own entrails and heart."[19] Sobrino is missing, however, that mercy is also a reaction to suffering of oneself; as a person experiences being wronged, hurt or victimized by an injustice, the person's reaction affects both parties.

Often, a distorted understanding of mercy—one closer to pardon— is the only option assumed. For the adolescent (and most people for that matter), this version of mercy is what the individual wants but often not what is extended. A sixteen-year-old breaks curfew and, on the drive home, rehearses a request for mercy. To let him off may seem to be merciful in the moment but may actually end in being harmful. Mercy moves beyond feeling, beyond emotion, and places praxis at the center of its existence.

Some take mercy as treating a person "less harshly than, given certain rules, one has a right to treat that person."[20] There are three elements present in this definition. One is that there is some concept of a right or just (albeit socially constructed) authority. Second, an individual has gone against or broken socially accepted forms of behavior or actions. Third, there is to be some form of compensation or proportionate action taken with regard to the wrongdoing.[21]

A person who has committed a crime may request mercy from the court. The court, by societal standards has every right to punish this person to the full extent of the law. If the court so chooses, the individual may be placed in prison for a set period of time. Part of the reality of this is that there are consequences not only for the wrongdoer but also for those related or attached in some significant way: is it just for a society to pay the bill for the keep of a wrongdoer, force a spouse to become a single parent, require a child to be without one or both parents? Is it merciful, then, to opt for strict probation rather than imprisonment? Might this type of mercy negate the worth of the original victim and the victim's family? Or might this type of mercy erode the

---

[19]Ibid.
[20]Jeffrie Murphy and Jean Hampton, *Forgiveness and Mercy* (New York: Cambridge University Press, 1994), p. 20.
[21]Ibid., p. 20.

societal pressure available to keep other people from committing similar wrongdoing? In this case, then, showing justice to the wrongdoer victimizes the wrongdoer's family, while showing mercy to the wrongdoer further victimizes the wrongdoer's victims.

Some define mercy derisively as absolution or the justification of wrong action. Many people who are outraged at violence in society, for example, will publicly sanction the death penalty as an act of justice, but it is difficult to imagine that even the strongest proponent of capital punishment would not seek mercy if the wrongdoer were a loved one. Justice, as it is most frequently dispensed, ignores factors of individuality; mercy is for the individual, however, and it takes time to get to know the person in the situation.

Some conceive of mercy as self-subordination. "Each would strive successful or unsuccessfully, to have other's interests preferred."[22] Internalizing the suffering of another is the foundation upon which mercy is built. Such mercy considers that an action has occurred for which an individual is either not responsible (a child being born into a plague-ridden or impoverished society) or for which the societally sanctioned consequence seems too harsh. Self-subordination means being able to admit that what seemed proportionately fair may, by the standards of mercy, in actuality be unjust.

In many Christian circles, mercy appears as the higher virtue over justice. And yet the sheer volume of work published on justice compared to the rather meager offerings on mercy is striking. No matter how one defines justice or mercy, they are not able to exist one without the other. And particularly in the very black-and-white world of early adolescence and the very self-focused world of middle adolescence, justice and mercy are experienced in relation to another person, group or institution. Individually or communally, adolescents will experience justice and mercy alternately as the recipient and the dispenser. A closer look at justice will help to clarify the relationship of coexistence.

---

[22]Garth Hallett, *Christian Neighbor-Love* (Washington, D.C.: Georgetown University Press, 1989), p. 120.

JUSTICE

Justice carries multiple understandings within multiple settings. Robert Nozick considers distribution of goods just if it occurs through a voluntary and fair process. This view does not consider whether the accepted system itself is fair; rather, the distribution is deemed fair if the system was followed. It is about the end results; the history of how something has come about is a moot point.[23] John Rawls looks more at the criteria of recipients, and distinguishes between social primary goods and natural primary goods; not only process but the history of the recipient and of the good are equally considered.[24] Alasdair MacIntyre states that "justice requires that we treat others in respect of merit or desert according to uniform and impersonal standards; to depart from the standards of justice in some particular instance defines our relationship with the relevant person as in some way special or distinctive."[25] "David Gil sees justice as "the absence of exploitation-enforcing domination; it implies liberty, while domination-induced injustice involves unequal, discriminatory constraints on liberty."[26] James Poling's definition builds a bridge to the most common understandings of justice: "the fair distribution of the resources needed for a full life."[27] Three questions immediately come to mind, however: (1) what is fair distribution? (2) what is a full life? and (3) who gets to decide either or both of these?

The nuances of Poling's definition can be teased out in at least three major variations: retributive justice, distributive justice and attributive justice. *Retributive justice* is what most commonly appears on the news or in the paper and apportions active punishment or deprivation of

---

[23]Robert Nozick, *Anarchy, State and Utopia* (New York: Basic Books, 1974), p. 11.

[24]John Rawls, *A Theory of Justice* (Cambridge, Mass.: Harvard University Press, 1971). Rawls requires an understanding of the recipients and goods. This invites the question, to which he responds for his entire book, of whether the recipient and goods have been correctly identified and defined.

[25]Alasdair MacIntyre, *After Virtue* (Notre Dame, Ind.: University of Notre Dame Press, 1984), p. 192.

[26]David Gil, *Confronting Injustice and Oppression: Concepts and Strategies for Social Workers* (New York: Columbia University Press, 1998), p. 10.

[27]James Newton Poling, *Render Unto God: Economic Vulnerability, Family Violence, and Pastoral Theology* (St. Louis, Mo.: Chalice Press, 2002), p. 205.

goods proportional to the actions of that person.[28] At an institutional level retributive justice directs certain feelings of anger, resentment and even hatred generally toward those who break the accepted norms or mores of a society. It states that a wrong has occurred and renders a proportionate consequence in order to vindicate the victim or teach the wrongdoer a lesson. Retribution forces a society to formalize what it will consider acceptable and what is out of the realm of acceptance. It is what, at least in part, constitutes a criminal justice system.[29]

Retributive justice assumes that all live within the understanding that "what is right for one person cannot be wrong for another similarly circumstanced. No one ought to apply a different standard to himself than to others if this in effect means that he accords himself a privileged position."[30] When a different standard is applied, injustice occurs. Under retributive justice, every person is to receive a standardized treatment, irrespective of the individual or the special relationship. It assumes a universal understanding of right and wrong as deemed by the structure and leading powers of society. This assumes, of course, that the leaders of that society are themselves seeking standards of equity for all and not adjusting the standards so as to place themselves in a position of privilege. A pure form of retributive justice is nearly impossible, if for no other reason than a difference of opinion occurs between leadership.

Retribution sounds punitive and consequently negative. It, however, is also the element of justice that provides for natural and logical consequences. The struggle comes in deciding what constitutes an injustice and what would be a suitable consequence. If a wrongdoer were to hit someone, one possible consequence would be to break the wrongdoer's hand or even to have it removed. Would it matter if this wrongdoer were seven years old as opposed to twenty-three? Would it matter if the wrongdoer had slapped someone on the back who was choking? According to our previous definition, justice is only justice if it disregards

---

[28]Paul Tillich, *Love, Power and Justice* (New York: Oxford University Press, 1967), p. 64.
[29]Murphy and Hampton, *Forgiveness and Mercy*, p. 2.
[30]Outka, *Agape*, p. 89.

any element of individuality. Consequences are to be established and rendered based on the action of the wrongdoer, regardless of the circumstances or ramifications.

Distributive justice is similar to retributive justice in that it is dependent on the actions of the individuals in accordance with the standards of society. It has a different slant on the societal perspective, however. "Distributive justice gives to any being the proportion of goods which is due to him."[31] If a person acts or reacts in accordance with the standards, she or he shall receive remuneration in proportion to the action offered as deemed appropriate by society.

Distributive justice attempts to have the same impartial treatment of the individual based solely on their merit or desert as retributive justice attempts. As distributive justice is based solely on the action of the individual, it is difficult to imagine a societal norm which supersedes the individual. And yet, this is exactly what distributive justice demands. It looks at the product, the end result, regardless of ability, age, skill or gifting. Distributive justice demands a blind eye as to the source with specific, consistent remuneration for specific actions.

This type of justice can be seen frequently in everyday incidents. The teenager at his first job in a fast food restaurant will earn the same wage as a college-educated, senior adult on her first job postretirement. Life experience, skills and need are not considered as long as the required tasks are completed satisfactorily. Children in school experience distributive justice all of the time. A child who struggles with English as a second language works toward the same passing grade in spelling as the native English speaker. The child who spends hours laboring over a science problem will receive the same grade as the student who completes the assignment in ten minutes (assuming they both arrive at the same answer). Distributive justice holds no regard for the individual; rather, the regard is for the standard.

In the very discussion of the merits of distributive justice comes one of its most basic refutations. Basing benefits solely in proportion to in-

---

[31]Tillich, *Love, Power and Justice,* p. 64.

dustry assumes that we live in a vacuum, that all people function with no regard for emotion or personal relationship. Instead, distributive justice presumes that people function on a cost-benefit business relationship. It sounds fair and equitable, and at least in theory, distributive justice eliminates any opportunity for discrimination—if benefits are based on industry alone, a woman who teaches a class for one hour will receive the same wage as a man teaching in the same school for one hour. But distributive justice has two problems.

First, distributive justice requires an ideal society that will abide by the rules necessary to make distributive justice work. All of society would have to disregard personal emotions, relationships and opinions; discrimination would have to cease to exist. This is a desired goal of many, but in order to achieve such a goal, all people would have to be willing to comply, at any cost. People might be lowered in status in order for more competent people to take their place. The toll this would take on those in power—even those who prefer to play the martyr—would be significant. More important, who makes the rules, and will they truly be ones in which distributive justice can exist?

Second, distributive justice requires the setting aside of personal preference. It would not be equitable to compensate a mystery writer more than an historical writer just because an individual opinion may value mystery more. It would not be just to compensate a human doctor more for one hour of labor than a veterinarian. Distributive justice requires a society of complete agreement, a society where all forms of work and creative endeavors are valued with no discrimination whatsoever. This sounds wonderful. The practicality and reality of it are merely fantasy.

The final of this trio, *attributive justice*, "attributes to beings what they are and can claim to be."[32] A high school basketball team is celebrated after returning home as champions. At a pizza party, each person starts with two slices, and the allocation of all further slices is based on each person's size. Justice in this form is perhaps the most influenced by the society in which it exists, which in turn makes it the most individualistic form of justice. An act of heroism in one location may be

---

[32]Ibid.

an act of treason elsewhere. The difficulty comes in the attempt to qualify adjectives. A man is a man. This can be shown to be fact. Whether the man is large or not is an opinion based on the person or society offering that description. Attributive justice attempts to bestow upon people what is rightfully theirs not by request but based on who they are and their value in that society. It attempts to afford the same opportunities to a child in the ghetto who plays piano as the child in the country club. It states that they may both be concert pianists given similar circumstances. Attributive justice seeks to acknowledge the individual and compensate or penalize based on the individual, not on a societal norm.[33] And yet, it is the accepted norms of society for an individual that delineates what is valued as an attribute.

Attributive justice attempts to acknowledge these differences, treat individuals based on their own merit within the greater confines of a particular society. In a caste system, all within the same caste are to be treated equally. In a patriarchal society, all men are treated in one fashion; all women are treated in another fashion. Different societies have different definitions of what is considered just. A society which values community over individuals would value a team which excels over an excellent individual player. Meanwhile, values change over time. In the United States, there was a time, now past, when a parent was considered just who used corporal punishment (in some cases even severe corporal punishment) on a child.

The question put to each of these three approaches to justice ultimately becomes, whose justice is just? Justice is a communally defined construct. Adolescents are constantly negotiating issues of justice, ranging from relationships to family roles. As Christians, we seek as best as we can to understand God's justice. The Bible offers some insight into this approach.

BIBLICAL VIEWS OF JUSTICE

Biblical views of justice offer different perspectives to a field dominated by distributive principles. It is first and foremost in line with what has

---

[33]Outka, *Agape*, p. 91.

already been established as the work of God in the world. Justice is "the order God seeks to reestablish in His creation where all people receive the benefits of life with Him."[34] Justice is not a passive concept; it carries action within its very existence. "God's justice may be expressed in deeds that liberate the weak and vulnerable from bondage as well as in judgment on the unfaithfulness of the people."[35]

God is relational, righteous and just. His acts are righteous and full of justice. His actions are in relationship to others. His justice is also tied to balance. It requires attention to detail in every arena. As Christians, our pursuit of justice must follow the same pattern.[36]

Part of our task as youth ministers is to express and model God's justice for and with our students, their families and our colleagues. Our acts ought to be righteous and full of justice. William Werpehowski points out that "the justice of human activity is measured by its faithfulness to the covenanting God, who may be identified in creation and history, in the Law and the Prophets, and ultimately for Christians, in the story of Jesus Christ."[37] Accepting this to be the case, justice is what occurs when we are following the relational example of God himself. It is not simply about the end but the history of both the recipient and the good in question, and more importantly, in relationship.

God's example of justice offers principles which can be translated into our present circumstances. Proverbs 2:9 looks systematically at the polis.

Then you will understand what is right and just
and fair—every good path.

Isaiah 11:4 looks at the oppressed:

With righteousness he will judge the needy,
with justice he will give decisions for the poor of the earth.

---

[34]*Holman Bible Dictionary* (1991), s.v. "Justice."
[35]R. K. Harrison, *Encyclopedia of Biblical and Christian Ethics* (Nashville: Thomas Nelson, 1992), p. 330.
[36]Amy Jacober, "Balance and Justice: A Youth Ministry Perspective," *The Journal of Student Ministries* (2008).
[37]Harrison, *Encyclopedia*, p. 330.

He will strike the earth with the rod of his mouth;
　　with the breath of his lips he will slay the wicked.

Isaiah 33:15-16 looks at what is just or righteous and the benefits of
living so.

Those who walk righteously
　　and speak what is right,
who reject gain from extortion
　　and keep their hands from accepting bribes,
who stop their ears against plots of murder
　　and shut their eyes against contemplating evil—
they are the ones who will dwell on the heights,
　　whose refuge will be the mountain fortress.
Their bread will be supplied,
　　and water will not fail them.

Acts 28:4-5 looks at consequential actions.

When the islanders saw the snake hanging from his hand, they
said to each other, "This man must be a murderer; for though he
escaped from the sea, the goddess Justice has not allowed him to
live." But Paul shook the snake off into the fire and suffered no ill
effects.

Justice is the standard by which penalties are assigned for wrongdoing. It is equally if not greater so that justice is the standard by which
advantages are handed out, including "material goods, rights of participation, opportunities and liberties."[38] A variety of words throughout
the Scriptures, all of which are heavily laden with meaning and nuanced in several ways, are all translated "justice." This alone shows
more than one application and correct understandings of justice. The
difficulty continues when looking closer at each example and the implications which naturally follow.

Shalom is a unique contribution of the biblical understanding of justice. Shalom has a much thicker meaning than its typical English

---

[38] *Holman Bible Dictionary* (1991), s.v. "Justice."

translation of "peace." Perry Yoder offers three fundamental features to the meaning: (1) physical well being, including adequate food, clothing, shelter and wealth; (2) a right relationship between and among people; and (3) the acquisition of virtue, especially honesty and moral integrity.[39] Shalom cannot exist in the absence of one or the other of these three. As the goal for justice, it is in line with aforementioned understandings of justice, but its relation is difficult to detect without first looking at the Hebrew expressions of righteousness and justice. This makes the discussion of shalom within the realm of justice much more crucial for the Christian believer; it is in opposition to much of the world, where more commonly the end is the goal.

Shalom opens the possibility that what is just is more than simply following standards already set in place. Rather, the standards, the relevancy of definition of both the recipient and good, are taken into account. Subsequently, shalom is sought both in the process and conclusion. This may mean unequal distribution, which to some would seem unjust. In this sense, the very state of justness begs a foundation in Christ over any other theoretical approach (though other theoretical approaches may be useful and helpful to the Christian both in seeking a greater understanding of justice and in dialogue with those outside of Christianity as well).

A Christian simply cannot look at justice in the same way as the world. We can neither overlook injustice nor simply seek more equal distribution. "For the true prophets, injustice was presumably, the opposite of shalom since it not only brought oppression but material want and deceit as well."[40] The biblical view of justice calls us to a higher understanding. That higher understanding is expressed by Perry Yoder: "God's justice is not thought of as the way of arriving at a decision pronouncing someone guilty or innocent. Rather, God's justice is an act which aids those in distress. . . . Justice is for the weak and oppressed

---

[39]Perry Yoder, *Shalom: The Bible's Word for Salvation, Justice and Peace* (Winnepeg: Faith and Life Press, 1987), p. 130.

[40]Perry Yoder, *The Meaning of Peace* (Louisville, Ky.: Westminster John Knox, 1992), p. 24.

and meant deliverance. To judge me means to vindicate me."[41] Retributive, attributive and distributive justice give according to desert; shalom justice gives according to need. Shalom justice clears the path to the righteousness of God without compromising his holiness and fully recognizing our brokenness. It removes the focus from the individual and replaces it with a focus on God.

By his very life, teachings and passion, Christ transforms the lives of the people around him and the relationships between them. Jesus, teaching to a crowd on the mountain, reverses the *lex talionis.* "An eye for an eye and a tooth for a tooth."

> I say to you, do not resist an evildoer. But if anyone strikes you on the right cheek, turn the other also; and if anyone want to sue you and take your coat, give your cloak as well; and if anyone forces you to go one mile, go also the second mile. (Matthew 5:38-41)

Jesus teaches shalom as the ultimate goal, God's intent for the community or society. It is in community that the weak are to be strengthened by the strong. It is in community where those who lack are provided for by those with plenty. Restoration to right relationship with God is the ultimate community. His justice takes a communal approach to each individual with eternal significance. The transformation of the individual within community occurs within the shift from justice as determined by distribution to justice as determined by the end result of shalom. This is not only a viable approach for youth ministry but allows for authentic and distinct ministry, not simply another youth organization.

MERCY AND JUSTICE: THE PATH TO RESTORATIVE AND TRANSFORMATIVE JUSTICE

Jeffrie Murphy states that "most of us do see justice as the primary virtue with respect to law, but we also want to find someplace for mercy as a secondary virtue to temper or otherwise have some effect on justice."[42] Between justice and mercy, the latter is often viewed as the kinder of

---

[41]Ibid., p. 33.
[42]Murphy and Hampton, *Forgiveness and Justice*, p. 182.

the virtues—but almost as a younger sibling which must be tolerated, not embraced. Justice and retribution, Murphy contends, are not nearly so evil as first assumed, and mercy is not nearly so benevolent.[43] Nuanced further, it might be said that neither justice nor mercy is purely malicious or benevolent apart from the another. Mercy is not needed to *temper* justice, and justice is not needed to *chasten* mercy; rather, each needs the other to truly *exist*. Justice could not exist apart from the individuals who constitute society. Mercy would cease to exist as a choice for the individual if the individual were no longer a part of the greater society.

Mercy, like all virtues, can have a negative side. Mercy run amuck would negate the trauma victims' suffering by allowing the wrongdoer to experience no external consequences. A parent motivated by mercy to impose no consequences on a failing teenager because he is "old enough to take care of himself" leads to more damaging results than had the parent exercised justice. One of my former ninth-grade students was frequently smoking marijuana. I let her parents know, and one of them quoted to me Proverbs 22:6: "Train up a child in the way he should go. Even when he is old he will not depart from it." As we talked, they told me they believed being merciful was the best way to communicate their love for their daughter. They had done their job in introducing their daughter to Jesus and the church and in providing a roof over her head. As a thirteen-year-old, it was now her responsibility to make life choices; she would be held accountable in life. She went on to abuse other drugs, become sexually active and then sexually promiscuous. For the adolescent, mercy and justice are difficult to interpret; the fine line between what is unjust and what is simply unfair or, even more, a consequence of an action is often difficult to determine. The deeper they are able to experience God's love, however, the more truly they are able to identify issues of justice and mercy in their own world.

Ultimately the only perfect marriage of mercy and justice has been in the life of Jesus Christ. The redemptive work of God was "intended to

---

[43]Ibid., p. 184.

benefit the whole world" and yet saves one individual at a time.[44] God is just—concerned that all receive what they deserve—and yet God is patient, offering what they will never deserve. God requires responsibility in the Christian life, and yet the mercy God offers delivers them from the harsh treatment they deserve. This is not a mercy with which he is stingy; it is a mercy meant for all regardless of past behavior, injustices inflicted or injustices suffered. He offers reconciliation, mercy and absolution. The concept that God desires that none should perish, taken seriously, means that God desires that all should know his mercy intimately and individually.

This same mercy he desires all to know individually becomes the point of commonality from which society exists. In this sense, once again, God's mercy taken to its extreme leads society to justice. It would be a society where others would be considered more highly than the self and therefore needs met, individuals honored and consequences administered justly. Taken in this way, justice can move far beyond the initial categories of retributive, distributive and attributive. Howard Zehr offered an alternative route with the systematic introduction of restorative justice.[45]

Restorative justice begins with a focus on the victims within a wrongdoing. It focuses on roles and needs of both the victim and the offender. Zehr would say that "restorative justice focuses on needs more than deserts."[46] Early on Zehr saw retributive and restorative justice as polar opposites, but he has since shifted his position; they in fact have many of the same goals, though the path each chooses to attain those goals is very different.

Restorative justice is primarily concerned with crime, but the principles are transferable to broader justice concerns. Zehr insightfully observes that within restorative justice, the victim and offender have the possibility of transformation within their lives. Restoration calls us to

---

[44]Clark Pinnock, *A Wideness in God's Mercy* (Grand Rapids: Zondervan, 1992), p. 17.
[45]Howard Zehr, *Changing Lenses: A New Focus for Crime and Justice* (Scottdale, Penn.: Herald Press, 1990).
[46]Howard Zehr, *The Little Book of Restorative Justice* (Intercourse, Penn.: Good Books, 2002), p. 18.

look to individuals within a society, to listen to prophetic voices, and be called collectively to a greater level of equality and justice. "Were critical consciousness to spread widely among significant majorities of people, from local to global levels, humankind could eliminate prevailing conditions of injustice and oppression."[47]

The work of God in the word is reconciliation. He is seeking to transform us individually, consequently allowing transformation to occur communally. This process is not linear and is certainly difficult to separate cleanly, but the interwoven, cyclical nature of our narratives draws us indefinitely closer to God. The mercy of Christ is aimed at restoring community between an individual and God for eternity. The shalom justice of Christ is aimed at restoring community right here and now by meeting the needs of individuals within community.

Youth ministry in general has not spent much time thinking through issues of love, justice and mercy in relation to one another. As with all areas of life the pressures of balancing many expectations have placed most ministers in a survival mode, focusing on the majority and often never noticing any who may fall on either end of the bell curve. Yet youth ministers are not void of thought, rather void of language and impetus to carve out time to begin thinking through situations in light of Christian ethics. Roger Nishioka offers a glimpse at the issue of justice:

> Sometimes leaders, seeking justice, make decisions on the basis of treating everyone the same way. This after all, is a common notion of fairness in our culture. Thanks be to God that God does not treat us fairly.
>
> Justice and fairness are not the same thing. God looks at each heart to know what we need. Grace is not bound by precedent or the need to view everyone the same way. Grace applies to each person individually as the Holy Spirit works with us in our uniqueness. One common complaint from young people is that adults often fail to see the individual; they just see a group of "kids." As youth ministers, we must take time to appreciate and consider the

---

[47]Gil, *Confronting Justice and Oppression*, p. 49.

needs of each young person as an individual.[48]

While certainly the individual is never to be lost sight of, there are times when a greater systemic issue is at hand. Youth ministry is rarely just about youth; it includes concern for broader issues such as a particular drug gaining popularity in a community; parents being preoccupied with their busy adult lives; performance pressure on adolescents from parents living vicariously through their achievement; and others. Meanwhile adolescents are in a period of change. The way an adolescent behaves on one day may not be how they behave on the following day. They are not certain what to do with themselves as they are barraged with mixed messages from the world every day. In other words, they are inconsistent—in developmentally appropriate and culturally understandable ways.

The challenge for adults and youth ministers in particular is to teach them as they are developing and growing what it means to know and be known by love, and fidelity from and for God. Indeed, by the very nature of adolescence, fidelity, transcendence (deep significance) and communion (intimacy) are innate longings born out of their passion and offer a natural point of connection with the passion of Christ.[49] Jesus loves them, we tell them, even as they wonder why their parents do not. The deep wounds that are left on the young by harsh spoken and unspoken messages cannot be underestimated, but they do not have to define them. Transformation through reconciliation is possible.

Even a child understands there are natural and logical consequences for actions. Transformative justice resulting in shalom will require far more. "Evidences are that we are holding very young children accountable for too much and not holding adults, who have professed Christ, accountable for enough."[50] God does not expect that we already know

[48]Rodger Noshioka, "Theological Framework for Youth Ministry: Grace," in *Starting Right: Thinking Theologically About Youth Ministry*, ed. Kenda Creasy Dean, Chap Clark and Dave Rahn (Grand Rapids: Zondervan/YS Academic, 2001), p. 251.

[49]Kenda Creasy Dean presents a detailed and convincing discussion of adolescents longing for fidelity. Kenda Creasy Dean, *Practicing Passion: Youth and the Quest for a Passionate Church* (Grand Rapids: Eerdmans, 2004).

[50]Clifford Ingle, ed., *Children and Conversion.* (Nashville: Broadman Press, 1970), p. 97.

how to behave in a just way. As youth ministers, we may be the only voice during an adolescent's formative years offering an alternative to the harsh and punitive world. Gary Haugen says, "As God calls us to seek justice, He bids us to equip ourselves with some basic knowledge of what it takes to pursue the call with excellence. He does not presume that we are ready but beckons us, 'learn to do right! Seek justice, encourage the oppressed. Defend the cause of the fatherless, plead the case of the widow."[51]

As much as the Christian world has struggled with this issue, the secular world is familiar as well.

> As originally conceived in 1899, the juvenile court sought to protect children from the impersonal legal processes of adult courts. Instead of an adversary approach, the child was to be offered the friendly help of a fatherly judge who would see to the individualized treatment and, if necessary, rehabilitation. Seventy years of experience with juvenile courts had demonstrated that the services for rehabilitation were a myth. In practice, the pretext of service was a substitute for justice. Children were incarcerated for indefinite periods. . . . In 1967 the Supreme Court decided children in trouble with the law had legal rights . . . the child court could have both, justice and service.[52]

When a child or adolescent has done wrong, are they strictly the oppressor or do they fall into a distinct category? And if they warrant their own category, who decides exactly what this will look like and how it should be handled? The court system has set a chronological age to differentiate between the adult and adolescent. In youth ministry, it is not nearly this clear cut. Youth ministers ask almost daily: do I give mercy or what is just?

Where the cultural context supports retributive justice as the norm, the theologically aware Christian youth minister awakens to new

---

[51]Gary Haugen, *Good News About Injustice: A Witness of Courage in a Hurting World* (Downers Grove, Ill.: InterVarsity Press, 1999), p. 144.
[52]June Axinn and Herman Levin, *Social Welfare: A History of the American Response to Need* (New York: Longman, 1982), p. 252.

understandings, ultimately ushering in shalom justice, leading to transformation and reconciliation. For shalom justice to occur, the presence
of mercy is required. The developmentally appropriate growth in pref-
erential love can be directed toward mutuality and the equal regard of
agapē. Above all, these three virtues offer the grounding for developmental growth in authentic communal relationships and the eternal
relationship of being a follower of Christ.

As an adolescent experiences the love of God and his transformative
justice, shalom occurs. Creasy Dean reminds us that "practices do not
transform us; *grace* transforms us. . . . Practices are trail signs, left by
generations of Christians who have gone before us, that point the way
to the cross—reminders that in dying to self there is new life."[53] As
youth ministers, it is our job to once again ask, "How do I best allow
God to work through me to bring about reconciliation? To bring about
transformation?"

It is not our acts, our practices, that bring the transcendent change.
Many youth workers have accepted the invitation of God to fully participate in his reconciliation. Even more, many youth workers have invited young people far beyond, experiencing God's love through community and in turn offering mercy that otherwise would have been
impossible. For others, however, we stop short of aiding adolescents to
be fully included. We begin to see adolescents who offer, quite imper-
fectly but authentically (not unlike ourselves), what God is doing in
their lives, and it does not look the way we expected. Adolescents have
an uncanny way of simply following Jesus, having not yet learned all of
the proprieties of being a Christian in our world today. Calenthia
Dowdy sees these adolescents in the role of prophet, and not just for
their peers. "Current youth ministry must release and empower its
young prophets, encouraging them to speak and act regarding both
moral and social righteousness . . . guide them as they ask hard questions. . . . It is a call to the *whole gospel*."[54] Fernando Arzola further
strengthens this position in seeking a Christ-centered, holistic, pro-

---

[53]Creasy Dean, *Practicing Passion*, p. 151.
[54]Calenthia S. Dowdy, "Voices from the Fringes: A Case for Prophetic Youth Ministry," *Journal of Youth Ministry* 3, no. 2 (Spring 2005): 95.

phetic youth ministry, where individuals and communities are considered for eternal or kingdom purposes.[55]

Youth ministry needs justice. Events occur every day, some large, some not so large. Adolescents, more acutely than at other developmental stages, are still learning and seeking connection across the chasm.[56] To walk alongside them, to guide them in experiencing the love of God and in recognizing moments of transformative justice in their lives, is part of the role of a youth minister which is too often neglected.

QUESTIONS FOR FURTHER THOUGHT

1. Where have you experienced the four types of justice in life (attributive, distributive, retributive and restorative)? How did this relate to your faith?

2. How do you understand the relationship between justice and mercy? How can you pass this on to teenagers?

3. In what ways does youth ministry model and help adolescents experience love, justice and mercy? What is the role of the Holy Spirit in this?

4. What is the relation between love, justice and mercy to the practical theology approach offered in this book? How does it apply to youth ministry?

---

[55]Fernando Arzola, "Four Paradigms of Youth Ministry in the Urban Context," *Journal of Youth Ministry* 5, no. 1 (Fall 2006): 53.

[56]James Loder reminds us that the negation of the negation can only occur by the power of the Holy Spirit. It is God's desire to bring about reconciliation, to turn the terror of the chasm into a transcendent eternal experience of faith, trust and belief.

7

TOWARD A MORE INTENTIONAL TRANSFORMATIVE MINISTRY

If you're lucky enough to find a way of life you love,

you have to find the courage to live it.

A PRAYER FOR OWEN MEANY

The future enters into us, in order to transform itself in us, long before it happens.

RANIER MARIA RILKE

Love has a hem to her garment

That reaches the very dust

It sweeps the stains

From the streets and lanes,

And because it can, it must.

MOTHER TERESA

THE PRIVILEGE AND PLEASURE for any youth minister is the imperative to join God in his work of reconciliation. This book has sought to develop a template to deepen a youth ministers' understanding of God's imperative as more than an invitation. While it is possible to do youth "work" apart from practical theology as God moves where he chooses, I contend that youth "ministry" is more likely to occur within the intentional focus created by practical theology. The alternative monolingual approach, which focuses on cultural issues, neglects crucial, indispensable areas of the adolescent life: an understanding of adolescent development and a construction of a theological framework.[1] A bilingual approach using both theological and psychosocial disciplines in dialogue, working together and informing each other, is crucial. While this bilingual approach requires greater effort, the consequences have eternal implications.

A BILINGUAL APPROACH

The first hypothesis that guided this work was *a bilingual conversation between theological and psychosocial perspectives,* which allows for focused consideration of theoretical and practical issues in the crucial passage from childhood to adulthood. The incarnation provides the precedent for the bilingual development of a practical theology: as Christ was both fully divine and fully human, so too, as we seek to imitate him, must be the dialogue we carry on in this world.

This bilingual dialogue recognizes the intertwined elements of the human and spiritual existing in each person. The spiritual is addressed in theological language, while the human is addressed in psychosocial language. The psychosocial is comprised equally of a developmental and cultural understanding. All of this and its integration is needed when looking at our identity development, in particular our identity in Christ. In order to be fully effective, addressing the appropriate developmental stage is necessary. In the life of teenagers, this requires a keen awareness of holistic adolescent development.

The template constructed here has more general applications than youth ministry alone. While one language in the bilingual conversation is always to be that of theology, the second language is determined by both the experience and the exploration phases of the pastoral cycle, raising questions to be answered in light of theological understandings.

---

[1]Discussions of cultural issues surrounding race, ethnicity and gender are likewise extraordinarily important, though space does not allow the consideration here that they deserve.

An event occurs, exploration takes place, reflection is required, and action is taken not based on impulse or uninformed choices but through careful consideration of a situation's "thickness" and with an eye toward transformation and reconciliation. It is a flexible template applicable to any ministry; it calls for ministry to remain Christian indeed and not slip into mere civic religion.

Each event in the pastoral cycle is enveloped in the grander encompassing narrative that comprises the life story of individuals and communities. As adolescents are in a transitional season of life—they are changing biologically, cognitively, emotionally and spiritually—the bilingual conversation has individual, communal and eternal dimensions.

The second hypothesis that has guided this work states that a practical theology of youth ministry *unites these three strands of existence:* the individual, the communal and the eternal. While each strand is unique and distinct, all three are considered in their distinction *and* their correlation.

One final hypothesis hones this practical theology template to a distinctly Christian position. In a Christocentric practical theology of youth ministry, *the virtues of love, justice and mercy manifest in the individual, communal and eternal,* informing one another in nurturing the maturing adolescent through the transformative power of Christ. It is not the youth pastor or the ministry that transforms an adolescent's life. It is our privilege to join God in his reconciling work as the adolescent experiences love individually, justice in community and mercy for eternity. It is through none other than Jesus Christ and his transformative power that this is possible, plausible and probable.

EVERYDAY EVENTS AS NARRATIVE

Every person encounters events each day that create the narrative of his or her life. Each of these events is a miniature narrative standing on its own. These narratives exist within the sovereignty of God. Apart from what we understand, we are living in the mystery of God's *telos* for this world. His connecting narrative, whether realized or accepted by the individual or not, reigns for eternity.

Practical theology orders these human narratives, offering the possibility of an intentional means of moving from the experience to action that goes deeper than a habitual response. The Holy Spirit is present at the event and throughout the pastoral cycle. We can invite his influence, grounded in the incarnation, as action is determined and implemented. Each narrative ideally will build on and learn from the last, moving us ever forward toward maturity, reconciliation and transformation. These narratives find their home in relation to the stories of others in community as they interlock and weave, creating a complicated tapestry.

With each narrative, a greater depth of understanding is acquired. With each narrative, praxis is shifted. Sometimes this is slight and sometimes it is great. For youth ministry and other areas, praxis is developed from both experience and reflection. It flows from what has gone before. N. T. Wright offers an analogy for considering an appropriate response to the authority of Scripture that finds equal application in practical theology.

> Suppose there exists a Shakespeare play whose fifth act has been lost. The first four acts provide, let us suppose, such a wealth of characterization, such a crescendo of excitement within the plot, that it is generally agreed that the play ought to be staged. Nevertheless, it is felt inappropriate actually to write a fifth act once and for all: it would freeze the play into one form, and commit Shakespeare as it were to being prospectively responsible for work not in fact his own. Better, it might be felt, to give the key parts to highly trained, sensitive and experienced Shakepearian actors, who would immerse themselves in the first four acts, and in the language and culture of Shakespeare and his time, *and who would then be told to work out a fifth act for themselves.*

Consider the result. The first four acts, existing as they did, would be the undoubted "authority" for the task in hand. That is, anyone could properly object to the new improvisation on the grounds that this character or that character was now behaving inconsistently, or that this or that subplot or theme, adumbrated earlier, had not reached its proper resolution. This "authority" of the first four acts would not consist of an implicit command that the actors should repeat the earlier parts of the play over and over again. It would consist in the fact of an as yet unfinished drama, which contained its own impetus, its own forward movement, which demanded to be concluded in the proper manner. But it would require of the actors a responsible entering into the story as it stood, in order first to understand how the threads could appropriately be drawn together, and then to put that understanding into effect by speaking and acting with both innovation and consistency.[2]

Each event in life may be new to the person at that moment, but it certainly is not the first time it has occurred. In fact, it may not be the first time it has occurred for that person. It is, however, the first time it has occurred with the amount of experience and reflection that one has at that precise moment. Practical theology ensures that we pay attention not only to the biblical narrative but to the life events that occur. In the words of the analogy, as those in youth ministry better understand the first four acts of the play, we may better know how to be consistent with the unknown fifth. With each new event, we must again reconsider the four acts.

INVITING YOUTH MINISTRY TO THE TEMPLATE OF PRACTICAL THEOLOGY

Youth ministry has a place in this dialogue. My focus has been honed within the bilingual conversation assuming the second language to be psychosocial and discovering what this means within the adolescent life stage. In this way, youth ministry is able to join with the wider church taking into account specific needs at this life stage but not ignoring the elements making it distinctively Christian and not simply a youth club.

Practical theology maintains a thread of connection between each preceding event in life. For the youth minister, this requires the intentional work of thinking Christianly while looking at the pragmatic issues within each event. It necessitates that the youth minister not act in isolation. Reflecting on past events is the responsibility of the minister within community. Evaluation requires reflection not only on informa-

---

[2]N. T. Wright, "How Can the Bible Be Authoritative?" *Vox Evangelica* 21 (1991): 16.

tion gathered but on personal and communal convictions as well. Youth ministers must themselves be connected with the church in order to do the evaluation within the pastoral cycle. The larger church community prevents the inadvertent omission of evaluative perspectives. This falls within the task of the youth minister to find how she can best join God in the work of reconciliation. She must seek to connect (to reconcile) adolescents with God, their peers and the various generations present in the church. Ultimately, this connection is the response to one of the fundamental questions asked during the adolescent stage of life: Where do I belong?

INDIVIDUATION, NOT ISOLATION

Individuation is the central task during the adolescent stage of life. Ideally, non-linear forward movement toward reconciliation and transformation will occur. Adolescents are asking the questions Who am I? Do I matter? Where do I belong? Individuation takes place to greater and lesser degrees in community, impacting the ease and health with which a child moves to adulthood. Adolescence brings the first potential for cognitive comprehension that there is the possibility for the negation of self. This is a large part of what makes adolescence such a crucial time in the spiritual life of an individual. Adolescents are developmentally able to begin grappling with the possibility of God entering into their life, in particular through the crucifixion and resurrection of Christ leading to the eschaton, thus negating the negation—the work of reconciliation initiated by God in the world.

The individual, communal and eternal dimensions of humanity coexist, requiring lifelong transformation, which takes place within both realms of the bilingual conversation. Maturity will occur to greater and lesser degrees within the psychosocial aspects of life as an individual finds her place within community. Reconciliation is both the result of and the initiator of transformation brought on by the Holy Spirit. "Through Christ, God constitutes us individually as believers and corporately as a community of believers."[3] This is the work of God in the

---

[3]Stanley Grenz and John R. Franke, eds., *Beyond Foundationalism: Shaping Theology in*

world. Theology is the language used to better comprehend this work of reconciliation, leading to transformation within all three dimensions of human existence. It brings a profound depth to lifelong development.

Youth ministers model this lifelong development within community for their students. Individuation is one step toward maturity and differentiation. With each life event, individuals and communities have the possibility of transformation. God is constantly at work transforming, seeking reconciliation but not stopping there.

Kant and Buber reminded us earlier to seek the other, not as a means to an end but as ends in and of themselves. We as adults seek to join God in loving adolescents in response to the work God has done and is doing in our lives, not in order to "get" something for ourselves. This pattern, firmly established in adolescence, continues throughout life as the adolescent connects with the church.

NEGATION TO TRANSFORMATION

God's work has the possibility of negating the personal negation. An adolescent can choose to recognize God as he enters into this moment of the negation by authentically experiencing love as an individual within community. The realization that this loves flows from a source much greater than the other humans nearby is worked out in community with other humans and with God himself. Love is expressed as equal regard for others through the administering of justice and mercy. To be treated justly or with mercy is to experience authentic love. The experience of authentic love ideally evokes the ability and desire to respond to others with justice and mercy. With each event, transformation takes place, moving ever toward God.

This process has been complicated by the world in which adolescents currently live. There is an overall abandonment of adolescents by the adult community. Popular research presents a generation more savvy and informed than any in previous times; what is missing is the understanding that being exposed to adult situations and choices does not necessar-

---

a Postmodern Context (Louisville, Ky.: Westminster John Knox, 2001), p. 48.

ily make for mature, healthily individuated adolescents. As they are having to find their own networks they are pushing their true selves just below the surface of what most adults (and adult approaches to working with adolescents) are ever able to detect. To further complicate matters, adolescents themselves state beliefs in strong terms, but when asked to explain what they mean, ambiguity arises. It may be that they are not so much hiding who they truly are as they are simply unable to articulate in any clear fashion just what they mean. The journey to adulthood is taking longer within a culture repeatedly clamoring for isolation but desiring community. Millennials are loyal and seek belonging. If belonging is not found within the biological family, they will find it elsewhere. Most often, it is found within small groups of friends.

The millennial generation comes as a unique group with its own characteristics and values. Their desire for authentic connection, not the desire for relevance of a previous generation, must drive ministerial approaches within youth ministry. Millennials are also open to the spiritual side of life.[4] This makes the role of the church and youth ministry even more crucial at this dynamic stage in life. Adolescents are not wanting to push the world away, isolating themselves from family and community. Indeed, they are looking for others who will be authentically interested in who they are as they struggle to individuate. This is good news for the church acting in natural response to the transformative power of Christ as God has poured out his love for it. Youth ministers are called by God to be about ministry. Ministry is about connection, both adults connecting with adolescents and, more importantly, adolescents connecting with God and his community. Unlike any other time in recent history, connection is what many adolescents are seeking.

RECONCILIATION

Practical theology always asks the question How may I best join God in his work of reconciliation in the world? The response comes in varying forms unique to each situation. Regardless of the situation, how-

---

[4]Christian Smith and Melinda Denton, *Soul Searching* (New York: Oxford University Press, 2005), pp. 170-71.

ever, reconciliation through transformation is the goal. Love expressed in justice and mercy brings about transformation; the authentic encounter with love cannot allow an individual to remain the same.

As an individual is changed, no matter how slightly, so is the community changed. With each turn of the pastoral cycle, there is the possibility for transformation and reconciliation to occur. While this pattern is not the exclusive experience of adolescents, it is powerfully displayed in their world. As adults, we can remain distant and safe, answering questions not being asked, or we can dive into the adolescent world and become enveloped in the process of transformation, becoming transformed as well.

Ultimately, conciliation is our work; reconciliation is God's work. Nurturance is our task; individuation is each adolescent's task within the lifelong process of differentiation. Opening youthful eyes to choose wisely what is individual, covenant faithfully that which is communal, and commit their lives to all that is eternal is our calling. The mystery and wonder we experience as we see it occur is recognition of the transformative power of Christ.

APPENDIX A

CHALCEDON AND THE BILINGUAL CONVERSATION

THE FOURTH ECUMENICAL Council was held in 451 at Chalcedon after over a century of the church wrestling with the nature of Christ.[1]

In the first centuries of the Common Era the church was a more unified whole. The question of how humanity and divinity were joined in Jesus Christ was primarily discussed in the East; Christians in the West were more occupied with invasions and other pressing matters. The West was content reviving Tertullian's understanding "that in Christ there were two natures united in one person."[2]

Among the most prominent events surrounding the understanding and development of this issue were four meetings that took place between 325 and 451.[3] At the Council at Nicaea in 325 Apollinaris of Laodicea proposed that Jesus had a physical body but not a human intellect: "The Word of God played in him the role that the intellect or 'rational soul' plays in the rest of us."[4] An addition was made to the creed in Constantinople in 381. It was now stated that Jesus was born

---

[1]Stanley Grenz, *Theology for the Community of God* (Nashville: Broadman and Holman, 1994), p. 388.

[2]Justo L. Gonzalez, *The Story of Christianity*, vol. 1, *The Early Church to the Dawn of the Reformation* (San Francisco: HarperSanFrancisco, 1984), p. 252.

[3]For a closer look at the documents and issues surrounding these times two books will be helpful: Philip Schaff, ed., *The Creeds of Christendom: With a History and Critical Notes*, rev. David Schaff (Grand Rapids: Baker, 1985), 2:57-65; T. Herbert Bindley, *The Oecumenical Documents of the Faith*, 4th ed., rev. F. W. Green (London: Methuen, 1950).

[4]Gonzalez, *Story of Christianity*, p. 253.

"of the Holy Ghost and the Virgin Mary" to guard against Apolli-
narianism.[5]

The next chapter of controversy came also from Constantinople. In
428 Nestorius, of the Antiochene school, became patriarch. His concern was whether the Virgin Mary had borne God or borne Christ.
Often his question is associated with Mariology, but this was much less
about Mary than about trying to understanding Jesus.[6] Nestorius tried
to propose that "although Jesus' humanity came through Mary, His
divine element came solely from God, Mary bore a man who was the
vehicle of deity, but not God."[7] Using the language of Mary as *Chris-
tokos* ("bearer of Christ") instead of *theotokos* ("bearer of God"), "he was
affirming that in speaking of the incarnate Lord one may and must
distinguish between his humanity and his divinity, and that some of
the things said of him are to be applied to the humanity, and others to
the divinity."[8]

This did not settle well with Cyril, Nestorius's Alexandrian bishop.
He ensured the support of the West (who considered the doctrine of
two persons in Christ anathema) and of the emperors Valentinian III
and Theodosius II, and called an ecumenical council in Ephesus in
431.[9] This council agreed with Cyril and declared Jesus to be one person not two. What they did *not* determine was the actual nature of the
one person of Jesus, and a new controversy flowed from the ambiguity
of the Council at Ephesus.[10]

In seeking a corrective to Nestorius and not finding it in the statement of the ecumenical council at Ephesus, Eutyches offered his understanding of the nature of Jesus. Unable to accept Jesus being divided into two natures, he proposed that Jesus was of one nature, both
human and divine, which commingled and formed a third new nature. This became known as the monophysite heresy, in which the
incarnate life was a third substance, neither divine nor human, but in

---

[5]Bindley, *Oecumenical Documents*, p. 65.
[6]Gonzalez, *Story of Christianity*, p. 254.
[7]Grenz, *Theology for the Community of God*, p. 386.
[8]Gonzalez, *Story of Christianity*, p. 254.
[9]Ibid., p. 253.
[10]Grenz, *Theology for the Community of God*, p. 387.

which divinity had a clearly dominant role. This then led to the fourth ecumenical council, Chalcedon, in 451.[11]

Chalcedon became the watershed for all Christology up to the present day. After condemning what had taken place at the "robbers synod" in Ephesus, the council at Chalcedon opted not to create yet another creed but rather sought to define the faith. The resulting definition was obviously heavily influenced by extrabiblical sources, but it never claimed any less. Responding to what the bishops felt were dangerous doctrines and creeds, and emerging out of both careful thought and the climate in which it was crafted, the main point of Chalcedon was to preserve the incarnation, not to explain how it took place.[12] The document produced at Chalcedon reads as follows.

> We, then, following the holy Fathers, all with one consent, teach men to confess one and the same Son, Our Lord Jesus Christ, the same perfect in Godhead and also perfect in manhood; truly God and truly man, of a reasonable (rational) soul and body; consubstantial (coessential) with the Father according to the God head, and consubstantial with us according to the Manhood; in all things like unto us, without sin; begotten before all ages of the Father according to the Godhead, and in these latter days, for us and for our salvation, born of the Virgin Mary, the Mother of God, according to Manhood; one and the same Christ, Son, Lord, Only-begotten, to be acknowledged in two natures, inconfusedly, unchangeably, indivisibly, inseparably; the distinction of natures being by no means taken away by the union, but rather the property of each nature being preserved, and concurring in one Person and one Subsistence, not parted or divided into two persons, but one and the same Son, and only begotten, God the Word, the Lord Jesus Christ, as the prophets from the beginning (have declared) concerning him, and the Lord Jesus Christ himself has taught us, and the Creed of the holy Fathers has handed down to us.[13]

---

[11]Ibid., pp. 387-88.

[12]Gonzalez, *Story of Christianity*, p. 257.

[13]Philip Schaff, ed., *The Creeds of Christendom: With a History and Critical Notes*, rev. David Schaff (Grand Rapids: Baker, 1985), 2:62-63.

The document produced in Chalcedon by no means put an end to christological debates, but it did change the playing field. There were of course those who hearkened back to the beliefs of Nestorius and those who held tightly to a monophysitic belief, but for the West and most of the East, Jesus was indeed understood as fully divine and fully human, with a rational soul and body—"at the same time of the same reality (or same essence) as us *(homoousion hemin)* as regards his humanity; like us in all respects, apart from sin."[14]

---

[14]Peter C. Hogsdon and Robert H. King, *Readings in Christian Theology* (Minneapolis: Fortress, 1985), p. 210.

APPENDIX B

VARIOUS PERSPECTIVES ON CULTURE

IT WOULD BE POSSIBLE TO SPEND an entire book considering various angles and issues surrounding the topic of culture. As a book solely on youth culture is not the intent, a select and fairly narrow acceptance of an understanding of culture is employed in this work.

This understanding did not emerge *ex nihilo* but rather evolved from long and varied paths of consideration. A full history of the development of culture either from a secular philosophical perspective or from a Christian perspective will not be presented here. What will be offered is a brief cogitation of major contributions.

It would be remiss to not first acknowledge the contribution of H. Richard Niebuhr in *Christ and Culture*, which borrows an understanding of culture from Bronislaw Malinowski and James Harvey Robinson. Niebuhr writes,

> What we have in view when we deal with Christ and culture is that total process of human activity and that total result of such activity to which now the name *culture*, now the name *civilization*, is applied in common speech. (Robinson, p. 735 and Brinkman, p. 525) Culture is the "artificial, secondary environment" which man superimposes on the natural. It comprises language, habits, ideas, beliefs, customs, social organization, inherited artifacts, technical processes, and values. (Malinowski, p. 621 ff) This "social heritage," this "reality sui generis," which the New Testament

writers frequently had in mind when they spoke of "the world," which is represented in many forms but to which Christians like other men are inevitably subject, is what we mean when we speak of culture.[1]

He goes on to say culture is always social, is human achievement, and is a pluralistic temporal and material realization of values.[2]

Niebuhr is asking three questions: How do we wrestle with God? How do we wrestle with culture? And above all, how do we wrestle with these two seemingly incompatible elements? In response he offers five categories: (1) Christ against culture, a sense of Christ being in opposition to culture; (2) Christ of culture, an agreement of Christ and culture; (3) Christ above culture, a synthetic approach; (4) Christ and culture in paradox, a sense of polarity; and (5) Christ the transformer of culture, a conversionist point of view.

Paul Tillich offers an existentialist integrative, or holistic, look at culture. Using his method of correlation, theology proceeds by seeking the questions of society (the questions proposed by culture and answered with theology). He wrestles with living life before God in reality.[3]

Emil Brunner offers six points of looking at culture: (1) the *imago Dei*, by which we have the ability to know God; (2) general revelation; (3) preserving grace; (4) divine ordinance; (5) the point of contact, dependent on the formal image of God; and (6) the relation of grace to nature (does grace abolish or perfect nature?).[4]

Karl Barth is frequently associated with Emil Brunner for their colorful relationship with one another. Barth would say that Brunner's position is a classic precursor of what will become heresy. (He would certainly include his former colleague Tillich's position here, though he never said so explicitly; their contrasting views on culture make it easy

---

[1]H. Richard Niebuhr, *Christ and Culture* (New York: Harper Torchbooks, 1975), p. 32.
[2]Ibid., pp. 32-38. See also Craig A. Carter, *Rethinking Christ and Culture: A Post-Christendom Perspective* (Grand Rapids: Brazos, 2006).
[3]See Paul Tillich, *Systematic Theology* (Chicago: University of Chicago Press, 1967); Paul Tillich, *Theology of Culture* (New York: Oxford University Press, 1964).
[4]Emil Brunner, *Christianity and Civilization* (London: Nisbet, 1948).

to identify at least one point where they parted company.) Barth accepts Christ, and Christ alone, as the point of commencement for thinking about culture.[5]

Perhaps the most widely read and influential of books across disciplines is *Habits of the Heart,* which defines cultures as "dramatic conversations about things that matter to their participants." Religion in the United States is here seen as an individualistic civic occurrence transcending and impacting every area of culture.[6]

Peter Berger is well known for his works in the area of culture. In his book *Social Construction of Reality,* coauthored with Thomas Luckmann, they consider a worldview as reality in which an individual externalizes his perceptions, objectifies these perceptions and then internalizes the external reality they perceived. As a sociologist, Berger continues on to present a position of culture becoming ensconced in a community until such a time where one or more rebel against the sacred order. The culture is then upset, and a new reality replaces it.[7]

Other perspectives include Stanley Hauwerwas and William Willimon, who believe the church is called not to transformation but to offer an alternative to greater culture;[8] George Lindbeck, who views the religious narrative as trumping the cultural narrative, so that the Christian community is to determine beliefs rather than accepting the alien explication of the larger culture;[9] Kathryn Tanner, who views that culture is the way we do theology, so that the cultural narrative trumps any other

---

[5]For more on this see Karl Barth and Emil Brunner, *Natural Theology: Comprising "Nature and Grace" by Emil Brunner and the Reply "No!" by Karl Barth,* trans. Peter Fraenkel (London: Cantenary Press, 1946).

[6]Robert Bellah, Richard Madsen, William Sullivan, Ann Swindler and Steven Tipton, *Habits of the Heart: Individualism and Commitment in American Life* (Los Angeles: University of California Press, 1996), esp. p. 27.

[7]Peter Berger and Thomas Luckmann, *The Social Construction of Reality: A Treatise in the Sociology of Knowledge* (Garden City, N.Y.: Doubleday, 1966); Peter Berger, *The Sacred Canopy: Elements of a Sociological Theory of Religion* (Garden City, N.Y.: Doubleday, 1967).

[8]Stanley Hauerwas and Willliam Willimon, *Resident Aliens: A Provocative Christian Assessment of Culture and Ministry for People Who Know Something Is Wrong* (Nashville: Abingdon, 1989).

[9]George Lindbeck, *The Nature of Doctrine: Religion and Theology in a Postliberal Age* (Philadelphia: Westminster Press, 1984).

with no overarching metanarrative in existence;[10] and David Tracy, who believes theology must move beyond the walls of the church to connect with other academic disciplines and larger culture and society.[11]

---

[10]Kathryn Tanner, *Theories of Culture: A New Agenda for Theology* (Minneapolis: Fortress, 1997).

[11]David Tracy, *The Analogical Imagination: Christian Theology and the Culture of Pluralism* (New York: Crossroad, 1981).

ACKNOWLEDGMENTS

This book was written with much gratitude to God on more levels than I could convey. Gratitude for the opportunity to study, to teach and to be graced with unexpected setbacks that afforded me more time to better offer what exists in these pages. I have been surrounded by an amazing crowd of people who have been cheerleaders, questioners, inspirers and iron to sharpen my thoughts. For the clear evidence of their support, I acknowledge this book could never have been without them. That said, for any errors, flaws or incomplete thoughts, I take full responsibility.

The thoughts of this book began in my own adolescent experience of being loved as an individual, experiencing justice and mercy in community, and knowing in my bones that there was an eternal strand running through the rhythm of life. I have come to understand this as kingdom work and have enjoyed countless hours enveloped in this area.

The thoughts of this book were advanced during my time at Fuller Theological Seminary. Dr. David Scholer was the first to encourage me to publish and, in fact, kept after me until I acquiesced. For his persistence, I am forever grateful. Dr. David Augsburger met weekly with me to take scattered notes and thoughts, teaching me to weave them together for strength. He helped to make me better than I ever thought I could be. Dr. Chap Clark has an inspiring commitment to the field of youth ministry and taught me more through his actions than any words could ever afford. Thank you as well to my Truett colleague Roger Olson for reading the chapter on theological influences in my life. Your insights are always valuable.

The thoughts of this book were tested over the years as I served in various settings. First with Katie Blincoe in West Seattle's Young Life and then with students at Agape Christian Church in Pasadena, California. You will always be the church and the group that taught me about love in its rawest and purest form. I couldn't have done this without my spiritual sister, Joyce del Rosario, through Tuesday night talks on the drive home from youth group. Finally, two very different groups helped me to hone and refine my understandings, contributing heavily to rewrites. The first are the students at The Church Without Walls in Houston, Texas. I loved serving with you. The second is Young Life's Capernaum, led by my dear friend Nick Palermo.

The thoughts of this book were sharpened over time by experience and through conversations with colleagues. I found confidence through two women in particular, Pamela Erwin and Calenthia Dowdy, who encouraged me, listened to me and challenged me. They are extraordinary colleagues and even better friends. A few others over the years have spent time reading or discussing my work, pushing me to contribute something of worth to the field. To Len Kageler, Fred Arzola and Kenda Dean, I am grateful for talks over drinks in various locations around Manhattan and the world.

The details of this book were strengthened by a handful of others. My editor, Dave Zimmerman, was amazing, coming alongside me in the most perfect of ways. I was also blessed with students who read, discussed, and offered insights or questions. Thanks to my students at Truett Theological Seminary, and to Kristen Nielsen, Reuben Lashley and David Hanson in particular for the time and work they gave.

Finally, the thoughts of this book would not be possible without those closest to me. For my dear parents, brother and extended family, thanks for believing in me before I believed in myself. To Richard and Carolyn Vash, who became family over my years at Fuller. To KB and RR, for reading work that was not in your field simply because you are my best friends and the closest I will ever know to sisters. For my loving and skilled husband—your support is priceless, reminding me that this is how it is supposed to be. For my two darling daughters: each of you slept in my lap during various times of my writing, reminding me of the hope of each new generation. May the love, justice and mercy of Christ shape every day of your life.

BIBLIOGRAPHY

Adler, Mortimer, and Charles VanDoren. *How to Read a Book: The Classic Guide to Intelligent Reading*. New York: Touchstone, 1972.

Anderson, Hebert. "The Recovery of Soul." In *The Treasure of Earthen Vessels: Explorations in Theological Anthropology, in Honor of James N. Lapsley*. Edited by Brian Childs and David W. Waanders. Louisville, Ky.: Westminster John Knox, 1994.

Anderson, Ray. *The Shape of Practical Theology: Empowering Ministry with Theological Praxis*. Downers Grove, Ill.: InterVarsity Press, 2001.

Arnett, Jeffrey Jensen. *Adolescence and Emerging Adulthood: A Cultural Approach*. Upper Saddle River, N.J.: Pearson Prentice Hall, 2001.

Arnett, Jeffrey Jensen, and Lene Arnett Jensen. "A Congregation of One: Individualized Religious Beliefs Among Emerging Adults." *Journal of Adolescent Research* 17, no. 5 (September 2002): 452, 464.

Arzola, Fernando. "Four Paradigms of Youth Ministry in the Urban Context." *Journal of Youth Ministry* 5, no. 1 (Fall 2006).

————. *Toward a Prophetic Youth Ministry: Theory and Praxis in Urban Context*. Downers Grove, Ill.: InterVarsity Press, 2008.

Augustine. *Confessions*. Translated by Rex Warner. New York: Signet Classic, 2001.

Axinn, June, and Herman Levin. *Social Welfare: A History of the American Response to Need*. New York: Longman, 1982.

Ballard, Paul, and John Pritchard. *Practical Theology in Action: Christian Thinking in the Service of Church and Society*. London: SPCK, 1996.

Barber, Bonnie, Jacquelynne Eccles and Margaret Stone. "Whatever Happened to the Jock, the Brain, and the Princess? Young Adult Pathways Linked to Adolescent Activity Involvement and Social Identity." *Journal of Adolescent Research* 16, no. 5 (September 2001): 431, 450.

Barth, Karl, and Emil Brunner. *Natural Theology: Comprising "Nature and Grace" by Emil Brunner and the Reply "No!" by Karl Barth*. Translated by Peter Fraenkel. London: Cantenary, 1946.

Bellah, Robert, Richard Masden, William Sullivan, Ann Swindler and Steven Tipton. *Habits of the Heart: Individualism and Commitment in American Life*. Los Angeles: University of California Press, 1996.

Berger, Peter. *The Sacred Canopy: Elements of a Sociological Theory of Religion*. Garden City, N.Y.: Doubleday, 1967.

Berger, Peter, and Thomas Luckman. *The Social Construction of Reality: A Treatise in the Sociology of Knowledge*. Garden City, N.Y.: Doubleday, 1966.

Bindley, Thomas Herbert. *The Oecumenical Documents of the Faith*. 4th ed. Revised by F. W. Green. London: Methuen, 1950.

Blos, Peter. *The Adolescent Passage: Developmental Issues*. New York: International University Press, 1979.

Blustein, David, and Donna Palladino. "Self and Identity in Late Adolescence: A Theoretical and Empirical Integration." *Journal of Adolescent Research* 6, no. 4 (October 1991): 440.

Boles, Scott A. "A Model of Parental Representations, Second Individuation, and Psychological Adjustment in Late Adolescence." *Journal of Clinical Psychology* 5, no. 4 (1999).

Bonhoeffer, Dietrich. *The Cost of Discipleship*. New York: Touchstone, 1995.

Boorstin, Jon. *Making Movies Work: Thinking Like a Filmmaker*. Los Angeles: Silman-James Press, 1995.

Borgman, Dean. *When Kumbya Is Not Enough: A Practical Theology for Youth Ministry*. Peabody, Mass.: Hendrickson, 1997.

Brown, Warren S., Nancey Murphy and H. Newton Maloney, eds. *Whatever Happened to the Soul? Scientific and Theological Portraits of Human Nature*. Minneapolis: Augsburg Fortress, 1998.

Browning, Don S. *A Fundamental Practical Theology: Descriptive and Strategic Proposals*. Minneapolis: Fortress, 1996.

Brunner, Emil. *Christianity and Civilization*. London: Nisbet, 1948.

Buber, Martin. *I and Thou*. Translated by Walter Kaufman. New York: Charles Scribner's Sons, 1970.

Bultmann, Rudolf. *Jesus Christ and Mythology*. New York: Charles Scribner's Sons, 1958.

Burkett, Elinor. *Another Planet: A Year in the Life of a Suburban High School*. New York: HarperCollins, 2001.

Campbell, John T. "Self or No-Self: Is There a Middle Way?" *Journal of Pastoral Care* 53, no. 1 (1999): 8-9.

Caporeal, Linnda, and R. M. Baron. "Groups as the Mind's Natural Environment." In *Evolutionary Social Psychology*. Edited by Jeffrey Simpson and Douglas Kenrick. Mahwah, N.J.: Lawrence Erlbaum, 1997.

Carter, Craig A. *Rethinking Christ and Culture: A Post-Christendom Perspective*. Grand Rapids: Brazos, 2006.

Clark, Chap R. "Entering Their World: A Qualitative Look at the Changing Face of Contemporary Adolescence." *The Journal of Youth Ministry* 1, no. 1 (Fall 2002): 10.

———. *Hurt*. Grand Rapids: Baker, 2004.

Corey, Gerald. *Theory and Practice of Counseling and Psychotherapy*. 4th ed. Pacific Grove, Calif.: Brooks/Cole, 1991.

Craig, Grace J. *Human Development*. 7th ed. Upper Saddle River, N.J.: Prentice Hall, 1996.

Creasy Dean, Kenda. "X-Files and Unknown Gods: The Search for Truth with Postmodern Adolescents." *American Baptist Quarterly* 19, no. 1 (March 2000): 11, 17.

———. "The New Rhetoric of Youth Ministry." *Journal of Youth and Theology* 2, no. 2 (2003).

———. *Practicing Passion: Youth and the Quest for a Passionate Church*. Grand Rapids: Eerdmans, 2004.

———. *Almost Christian: What the Faith of Our Teenagers Is Telling the American Church*. New York: Oxford University Press, 2010.

Creasy Dean, Kenda, Chap Clark and Dave Rahn, eds. *Starting Right: Thinking Theologically About Youth Ministry*. Grand Rapids: Zondervan, 2001.

Detweiler, Craig. "The Holy Trinity of Filmmaking." Lecture at Fuller Theological Seminary, Pasadena, Calif., 2002.

Dowdy, Calenthia. "Voice from the Fringes: A Case for Prophetic Youth Ministry." *Journal of Youth Ministry* 3, no. 2 (Spring 2005).

Dowdy, Calenthia, Pamela Erwin and Amy Jacober. "A New Eden Identity." *Journal of Youth and Theology* 9, no. 2 (2010).

Elkind, David. *The Hurried Child: Growing Up Too Fast Too Soon*. 3rd ed. Cambridge, Mass.: Perseus, 2001.

Erikson, Erik. *The Life Cycle Completed*. New York: W. W. Norton, 1887.

Erwin, Pamela. *A Critical Approach to Youth Culture: Its Influence and Implications for Ministry*. Grand Rapids: Zondervan, 2010.

Ferrer-Wreder, Laura, et al. "Promoting Identity Development in Marginalized Youth." *Journal of Adolescent Research* 17, no. 2 (March 2002): 168-69.

Fletcher, Joseph. *Situation Ethics.* Philadelphia: Westminster John Knox, 1966.

Ford, David. *Self and Salvation: Being Transformed.* New York: Cambridge University Press, 1999.

Forrester, Duncan. *Truthful Action: Explorations in Practical Theology.* Edinburgh: T & T Clark, 2000.

————. *Theological Fragments: Explorations in Unsystematic Theology.* New York: T & T Clark, 2005.

Freeman, Curtis, James Wm. McClendon Jr. and C. Rosalee Velloso da Silva. *Baptist Roots: A Reader in the Theology of a Christian People.* Valley Forge, Penn.: Judson Press, 1999.

Freire, Paulo. *Pedagogy of the Oppressed.* Translated by Myra Bergman Ramos. New York: Continuum, 1989.

Gabig, Jack. *Youth, Religion and Film.* Cambridge: YTC Press, 2007.

Garland, Diana. *Family Ministry: A Comprehensive Guide.* Downers Grove, Ill.: InterVarsity Press, 1999.

Geertz, Clifford. *The Interpretation of Culture.* New York: Basic Books, 1973.

Gil, David. *Confronting Injustice and Oppression: Concepts and Strategies for Social Workers.* New York: Columbia University Press, 1998.

Godawa, Brian. *Hollywood Worldviews: Watching Films with Wisdom and Discernment.* Downers Grove, Ill.: InterVarsity Press, 2002.

Gonzalez, Justo L. *The Story of Christianity.* Vol. 1, *The Early Church to the Dawn of the Reformation.* San Francisco: HarperSanFrancisco, 1984.

Grenz, Stanley J. *Revisioning Evangelical Theology: A Fresh Agenda for the 21st Century.* Downers Grove, Ill.: InterVarsity Press, 1993.

————. *Theology for the Community of God.* Nashville: Broadman and Holman, 1994.

————. *A Primer on Postmodernism.* Grand Rapids: Eerdmans, 1996.

————. *Created for Community: Connecting Christian Belief with Christian Living.* Grand Rapids: Baker, 1998.

————. *The Social God and the Relational Self: A Trinitarian Theology of the Imago Dei.* Louisville, Ky.: Westminster John Knox, 2001.

————. "Community and Relationships: A Theological Take." *Talk: The Mainstream Magazine,* February 9, 2002. Accessed at <www.stanleyjgrenz.com/articles/talk_mag.html>.

————. "Concerns of a Pietist with a PhD." Address at the American Academy of Religion, Toronto, Ontario, November 23, 2002.

Grenz, Stanley, and John Franke. *Beyond Foundationalism: Shaping Theology in a Postmodern Context*. Louisville, Ky.: Westminster John Knox, 2001.

Grenz, Stanley, and Roger Olson. *20th-Century Theology: God and the World in a Transitional Age*. Downers Grove, Ill.: InterVarsity Press, 1992.

Haitch, Russell. "Trampling Down Death by Death." In *Redemptive Transformation in Practical Theology: Essays in Honor of James Loder*. Edited by Dana Wright and John Kuentzel. Grand Rapids: Eerdmans, 2004.

Hall, G. Stanley. *Adolescence: Its Psychology and Its Relation to Physiology, Anthropology, Sociology, Sex, Crime, Religion, and Education*, vols. 1-2. Englewood Cliffs, N.J.: Prentice-Hall, 1904.

Hallett, Garth. *Christian Neighbor-Love*. Washington, D.C.: Georgetown University Press, 1989.

Harrison, R. K. *Encyclopedia of Biblical and Christian Ethics*. Nashville: Thomas Nelson, 1992.

Hauerwas, Stanley. *A Community of Character: Toward a Constructive Christian Ethic*. Notre Dame, Ind.: University of Notre Dame Press, 1981.

Hauerwas, Stanley, and William Willimon. *Resident Aliens: A Provocative Christian Assessment of Culture and Ministry for People Who Know Something Is Wrong*. Nashville: Abingdon, 1989.

Haugen, Gary A. *Good News About Injustice: A Witness of Courage in a Hurting World*. Downers Grove, Ill.: InterVarsity Press, 1999.

Heidegger, Martin. *Basic Writings*. Translated by David F. Krell. San Francisco: Harper & Row, 1977.

Heitink, Gerben. *Practical Theology: History, Theory, Action Domains*. Grand Rapids: Eerdmans, 1993.

Hersch, Patricia. *A Tribe Apart: A Journey into the Heart of American Adolescence*. New York: Ballantine, 1999.

Hogsdon, Peter C., and Robert H. King, *Readings in Christian Theology*. Minneapolis: Fortress, 1985.

Howe, Neil, and William Strauss. *The Fourth Turning: An American Prophecy*. New York: Broadway Books, 1998.

————. *Millennials Rising: The Next Generation*. New York: Vintage, 2000.

Hunsinger, Deborah van Deusen. *Theology and Pastoral Counseling: A New Interdisciplinary Approach*. Grand Rapids: Eerdmans, 1995.

Hunsinger, George. *How to Read Karl Barth: The Shape of His Theology*.

New York: Oxford University Press, 1991.

Ingle, Clifford, ed. *Children and Conversion*. Nashville: Broadman Press, 1970.

Jackson, Allen. "Does the Church Need Youth Ministry?" *American Baptist Quarterly* 19, no. 1 (March 2000): 33, 41-42.

Jacober, Amy. "Balance and Justice: A Youth Ministry Perspective." *The Journal of Youth Ministries* (2008).

Jammer, Max. *The Conceptual Development of Quantum Mechanics*. New York: McGraw Hill, 1966.

Josselson, Ruthellen. "Identity and Relatedness in the Life Cycle." In *Identity and Development: An Interdisciplinary Approach*. Edited by Harke Bosma, Tobi Graafsma, Harold Grotevant and David deLevita. Thousand Oaks, Calif.: Sage, 1994.

Jung, Carl Gustav. *The Portable Jung*. Edited by Joseph Campbell. Translated by R. F. C. Hull. New York: Penguin Books, 1971.

Kant, Immanuel. *Groundwork of the Metaphysics of Morals*. Translated by H. J. Paton. San Francisco: Harper Torchbooks, 1956.

Kaplan, Louise J. *Adolescence: The Farewell to Childhood*. New York: Touchstone, 1984.

Kohut, Heinz. *The Search for Self: Selected Writings of Heinz Kohut, 1950-1978*. Edited by P. H. Ornstein. New York: International University Press, 1978.

———. *Self Psychology and the Humanities: Reflections on a New Psychoanalytic Approach*. Edited by C. Strozier. New York: W. W. Norton, 1985.

Kozol, Jonathan. *Amazing Grace: The Lives of Children and the Conscience of a Nation*. New York: Perennial, 2000.

LaCugna, Catherine Mowry. *God for Us: The Trinity and Christian Life*. San Francisco: HarperSanFrancisco, 1992.

LeBlanc, Adrian Nicole. *Random Family: Love, Drugs, Trouble and Coming of Age in the Bronx*. New York: Scribner, 2003.

Lindbeck, George. *The Nature of Doctrine: Religion and Theology in a Postliberal Age*. Philadelphia: Westminster Press, 1984.

Lipper, Joanna. *Growing Up Fast*. New York: Picador, 2003.

Livermore, David. "The Youth Ministry Education Debate: Irrelevant Theorists vs. Mindless Practitioners." *The Journal of Youth Ministry* 1, no. 1 (Fall 2002): 89-102.

Loder, James. *The Transforming Moment*. 2nd ed. Colorado Springs: Helmers & Howard, 1989.

————. "Incisions from a Two-Edged Sword." In *The Treasure of Earthen Vessels: Explorations in Theological Anthropology, in Honor of James N. Lapsley.* Louisville, Ky.: Westminster John Knox, 1994.

————. *The Logic of the Spirit: Human Development in Theological Perspective.* San Francisco: Jossey-Bass, 1998.

Loder, James, and James Fowler. "Conversations of Fowler's *Stages of Faith* and Loder's *The Transforming Moment.*" *Religious Education* 77, no. 2 (March-April 1982): 133-48.

MacIntyre, Alasdair. *After Virtue.* 2nd ed. Notre Dame, Ind.: University of Notre Dame Press, 1984.

Mahler, Margaret. "A Study of the Separation and Individuation Process." *The Psychoanalytic Study of the Child* 26 (1971): 403-22.

Marcia, James. "The Empirical Study of Ego Identity." In *Identity and Development: An Interdisciplinary Approach.* Edited by Harke Bosma, Tobi Graafsma, Harold Grotevant and David deLevita. Thousand Oaks, Calif.: Sage, 1994.

Marshall, Sheila. "Do I Matter? Construct Validation of Adolescents' Perceived Mattering to Parents and Friends." *Journal of Adolescence* 24 (2001): 474.

McBeth, Leon H. *The Baptist Heritage: Four Centuries of Baptist Witness.* Nashville: Broadman Press, 1987.

McClendon, James Wm., Jr. *Systematic Theology.* Vol. 1, *Ethics.* Nashville: Abingdon, 1986.

————. *Systematic Theology.* Vol. 2, *Doctrine.* Nashville: Abingdon, 1994.

————. *Types of Christian Theology.* Class Notes. Pasadena, Calif.: Fuller Theological Seminary, February 25, 1999.

————. *Systematic Theology.* Vol. 3, *Witness.* Nashville: Abingdon, 2000.

McClendon, James Wm., Jr., and James M. Smith. *Biography as Theology: How Life Stories Can Remake Theology.* Philadelphia: Trinity Press, 1990.

————. *Convictions: Defusing Religious Relativism.* Valley Forge, Penn.: Trinity Press International, 1994.

Meadows, Susannah. "Meet the GAMMA Girls." *Newsweek,* June 3, 2002, pp. 44-51.

Migliore, Daniel. *Faith Seeking Understanding: An Introduction to Christian Theology.* Grand Rapids: Eerdmans, 2004.

Minus, Paul M. *Walter Rauschenbusch: American Reformer.* New York: Macmillan, 1988.

Moltmann, Jürgen. *The Experiment Hope*. Translated by M. Douglas Meeks. Philadelphia: Fortress, 1975.

Mueller, Walt. *Youth Culture 101*. Grand Rapids: Zondervan, 2007.

Murphy, Jeffrie, and Jean Hampton. *Forgiveness and Mercy*. New York: Cambridge University Press, 1994.

Murphy, Nancey, Iain Torrance et al., eds. *Bodies and Souls, or Spirited Bodies*. New York: Cambridge University Press, 2006.

Nel, Malan. "Serving Them Back: Youth Evangelism in a Secular and Postmodern World." *Journal of Youth and Theology* 1, no. 1 (April 2002): 69-70.

———. "Youth Ministry: The Challenge of Individuation." Paper presented at the International Association for the Study of Youth Ministry. Oxford, England, January 2003.

Newman, Barbara, and Philip Newman. "Group Identity and Alienation: Giving the We Its Due." *Journal of Youth and Adolescence* 30, no. 5 (October 2001): 515-38.

Niebuhr, H. Richard. *Christ and Culture*. New York: Harper Torchbooks, 1975.

Nishioka, Rodger. "Theological Framework for Youth Ministry: Grace." In *Starting Right: Thinking Theologically About Youth Ministry*. Edited by Kenda Creasy Dean, Chap Clark and Dave Rahn. Grand Rapids: Zondervan/YS Academic, 2001.

Nozick, Robert. *Anarchy, State and Utopia*. New York: Basic Books, 1974.

O'Koon, J. "Attachment to Parents and Peers in Late Adolescence and Their Relationship with Self-Image." *Adolescence 32* (1997): 472.

Outka, Gene. *Agape: An Ethical Analysis*. New Haven, Conn.: Yale University Press, 1972.

Pannenberg, Wolfhart. *Systematic Theology*. 3 vols. Translated by Geoffrey Bromiley. Grand Rapids: Eerdmans, 1990.

Piaget, Jean. *The Child and Reality: Problems of Genetic Psychology*. New York: Penguin, 1977.

Pinnock, Clark. *A Wideness in God's Mercy*. Grand Rapids: Zondervan, 1992.

Plato. *The Republic*. Translated by Robin Waterfield. Oxford: Oxford University Press, 1993.

Poling, James Newton. *Render unto God: Economic Vulnerability, Family Violence, and Pastoral Theology*. St. Louis, Mo.: Chalice Press, 2002.

Poling, James N., and Donald E. Miller. *Foundations for a Practical Theology of Ministry*. Nashville: Abingdon, 1985.

Post, Stephen. "Love and the Deeply Forgetful." Lecture presented at Azusa Pacific University, Azusa, Calif., November 2005.

Postman, Neil. *The Disappearance of Childhood.* New York: Vintage, 1994.

Rauschenbusch, Walter. *Christianity and the Social Crisis.* New York: Macmillan, 1914.

———. *The Social Principles of Jesus.* New York: Gorsett and Dunlap, 1916.

———. *A Theology for the Social Gospel.* New York: Macmillan, 1918.

———. *Prayers of the Social Awakening.* Boston: Jordan and More Press, 1925.

———. *The Righteousness of the Kingdom.* Nashville: Abingdon, 1968.

———. *Dare We Be Christians?* Cleveland: Pilgrim Press, 1993.

Rawls, John. *A Theory of Justice.* Cambridge, Mass.: Harvard University Press, 1971.

Resnick, M. D., et al. "Protecting Adolescents from Harm: Findings from the National Longitudinal Study on Adolescent Health." *Journal of the American Medical Association* 278 (1997): 825.

Root, Andrew. *Revisiting Relational Youth Ministry.* Downers Grove, Ill.: InterVarsity Press, 2007.

Samuolis, Jessica, Kiera Layburn and Kathleen Schiaffina. "Identity Development and Attachment to Parents of College Students." *Journal of Youth and Adolescence* 30, no. 3 (June 2001): 374.

Santrock, John. *Adolescence.* 4th ed. Dubuque, Ia.: William C. Brown, 1990.

———. *Adolescence.* 11th ed. New York: McGraw-Hill, 2007.

Savage, Jon. *TeenAge: The Creation of Youth Culture.* New York: Viking, 2007.

Scalise, Charles. *Bridging the Gap: Connecting What You Learned in Seminary with What You Find in the Congregation.* Nashville: Abingdon, 2003.

Schaff, Philip, ed. *The Creeds of Christendom: With a History and Critical Notes,* vol. 2. Revised by David Schaff. Grand Rapids: Baker, 1985.

Schlosser, Eric. *Fast Food Nation: The Dark Side of the All-American Meal.* New York: Perennial, 2002.

Schneider, Barbara, and David Stevenson. *The Ambitious Generation: America's Teenagers Motivated but Directionless.* New Haven, Conn.: Yale University Press, 1999.

Schwartz, Seth. "A New Identity for Identity Research: Recommendations for Expanding and Refocusing Identity Literature." *Journal of Adolescent Research* (May 2005).

Sharpe, Dores Robinson. *Walter Rauschenbusch.* New York: Macmillan, 1942.

Smith, Christian, and Melinda Lundquist Denton. *Soul Searching: The Religious and Spiritual Lives of American Teenagers*. New York: Oxford University Press, 2005.

Smith, Christian, and Patricia Snell. *Souls in Transition: The Religious and Spiritual Lives of Emerging Adults*. New York: Oxford University Press, 2009.

Smucker, Donovan. *The Origins of Walter Rauschenbusch's Social Ethics*. Buffalo, N.Y.: McGill-Queen's University Press, 1994.

Sobrino, Jon. *The Principle of Mercy: Taking the Crucified People from the Cross*. New York: Orbis, 1994.

Solarz, Andrea. *American Psychological Association Healthy Adolescents Project: Adolescent Development Project*. Washington, D.C.: American Psychological Association, 2002.

Stackhouse, Max. "Rauschenbusch Today: The Legacy of a Loving Prophet." *Christian Century*, January 25, 1989.

Stone, Howard H., and James O. Duke. *How to Think Theologically*. Minneapolis: Fortress, 1996.

Tanner, Kathryn. *Theories of Culture: A New Agenda for Theology*. Minneapolis: Fortress, 1997.

Tillich, Paul. *Systematic Theology*, vol. 1. Chicago: University of Chicago Press, 1951.

———. *Systematic Theology*, vol. 2. Chicago: University of Chicago Press, 1967.

———. *Love, Power and Justice*. New York: Oxford University Press, 1967.

Tracy, David. *The Analogical Imagination: Christian Theology and the Culture of Pluralism*. New York: Crossroad, 1981.

Trujillo, Kelli. "Strategies for Reaching Today's Kids: Three Rules About Millennials." *Group Magazine*, January 2, 2002, pp. 49-52.

Turpin, Katherine. *Branded: Adolescents Converting from Consumer Faith*. Cleveland: Pilgrim, 2006.

Volf, Miroslav, and Dorothy Bass, eds. *Practicing Theology: Beliefs and Practices in Christian Life*. Grand Rapids: Eerdmans, 2002.

Wilkinson, Loren. "Culture." In *The Complete Book of Everyday Christianity*. Edited by Robert Banks and R. Paul Stevens. Downers Grove, Ill.: InterVarsity Press, 1997.

Willis, Paul. *Common Culture*. Boulder, Colo.: Westview, 1993.

Wittgenstein, Ludwig. *Philosophical Investigations*. Translated by G. E. M.

Anscombe. New York: Macmillan, 1953.

Woodward, James, and Stephen Pattison, eds. *The Blackwell Reader in Pastoral and Practical Theology.* Oxford: Blackwell, 2000.

Wright, Dana, with Kenda Creasy Dean. "Youth, Passion, and Intimacy in the Context of Koinonia." In *Redemptive Transformation in Practical Theology: Essays in Honor of James Loder.* Edited by Dana Wright and John Kuentzel. Grand Rapids: Eerdmans, 2004.

Wright, Dana, and John Kuentzel, eds. *Redemptive Transformation in Practical Theology: Essays in Honor of James Loder.* Grand Rapids: Eerdmans, 2004.

Wright, N. T. "How Can the Bible Be Authoritative?" *Vox Evangelica* 21 (1991): 7-32.

Yoder, John Howard. *For the Nations: Essays Public and Evangelical.* Eugene, Ore.: Wipf & Stock, 2002.

Yoder, Perry. *Shalom: The Bible's Word for Salvation, Justice and Peace.* Winnepeg: Faith and Life Press, 1987.

———. *The Meaning of Peace.* Louisville, Ky.: Westminster John Knox, 1992.

Zehr, Howard. *Changing Lenses: A New Focus for Crime and Justice.* Scottdale, Penn.: Herald, 1990.

———. *The Little Book of Restorative Justice.* Intercourse, Penn.: Good Books, 2002.

Index of Names and Subjects

Scripture Index